CORPORATION TRAMWAYS.
JACKSON A.M.I.A.E.

British Trolleybuses 1911-1972

U·1505

British Trolleybuses 1911-1972

Geoff Lumb

Contents

First published 1995

ISBN 0 7110 2347 6

Published by Ian Allan Publishing

an imprint of Ian Allan Ltd, Terminal House, Station Approach, Shepperton, Surrey TW17 8AS.
Printed by Ian Allan Printing Ltd, Coombelands House, Coombelands Lane, Addlestone, Weybridge, Surrey KT15 1HY.

Photographs :-
GLC = Geoff. Lumb Collection

Front cover:
Huddersfield No 575, a 1949 Sunbeam MS2, was rebodied by C. H. Roe in 1959. It is seen reversing on to the former turntable at Longwood. The vehicle remained in service until January 1965. *Author*

Back cover, top:
Mexborough & Swinton No 37, a 1950 Sunbeam F4 fitted with a Brush 32-seat centre-entrance body is seen negotiating the one-way system past Conisbrough Castle as it climbs to Conisbrough High in 1960. In 1961, after the closure of the system, it was sold to Bradford, entering service in December 1962 after being fitted with a new East Lancs 66-seat body. It remained in service until 26 March 1972. *Author*

Back cover, bottom:
Bournemouth No 300, a Sunbeam MF2B, was one of the last new trolleybuses to be placed in service in Britain. It entered service in September 1962 and was finally withdrawn in 1969. *Author*

Acknowledgements

The principal sources of material used for this book have been brochures issued by manufacturers and suppliers along with contemporary articles published in the trade press between 1905 and 1950.

These have been supplemented by information from the PSV Circle, courtesy of the Hon Editor D. I. Gray. Chris Taylor allowed access to the HCVC Library and to his own collection of manufacturers' records. David Beilby allowed access to a vast amount of material from the many electrical companies absorbed into the present GEC Alsthom Traction Ltd. John M. Aldridge was extremely helpful in loaning material and photographs which filled many gaps. Rosie Thacker at the National Tramway Museum, Crich, played an important part in allowing access to the museum's extensive library and in providing copies of countless articles and documents. The Managing Director of Clough, Smith Ltd, Mr A. P. Marshall, provided information which helped to unravel many of the early mysteries.

Others deserving mention are G. Atkins, R. Brook, Adam Gordon, D. Hurley, A. Ingram, R. Marshall, J. P. Senior, P. B. Smith, D. J. Smithies, and Mr Bottomley and the staff at the West Yorkshire County Archive, Wakefield. I am also grateful to the three readers of *Classic Bus* — H. T. Matthews, S. Philips and P. Sutherland — who loaned brochures after the editor's appeal.

Special thanks to my daughter Jane for her invaluable help in putting my script on to disk and to M. Bray, industrial photographer, who provided the professional skills to produce superb prints from negatives or photographs over 70 years old. I am also grateful to the publishers, Ian Allan Ltd, for their help in producing this book.

Last, but not least, to my wife Ethel for her patience when files, records and photographs for all the suppliers and users of trolleybuses cluttered up the house.

Foreword

by the Revd J. P. Senior, BSc (Eng)

I have childhood memories of the Leeds 'track-lesses', especially of the day (presumably in 1928) when they cut down the wires in my native village of Menston-in-Wharfedale. At school in Huddersfield from 1934 I listed the new red 'trolleybuses' as they arrived, cycled over each route as it opened… and decided that passenger transport should be my career! My ambition was realised when, after the war, I became a trainee at Huddersfield. Then I moved to St Helens where I had the job of cutting down some of their wires.

Now memory is not what it was, and notebooks are tattered. So I was delighted to hear that Geoff Lumb was collecting a new set of photographs of British trolleybuses and taking a fresh look at the many firms involved in their manufacture. Time for the extensive research needed became available during a period of unemployment, and Geoff deserves congratulation for making good use of it.

The outcome is *British Trolleybuses 1911-1972,* a quite different approach to the history of the trolleybus. By a new author and with much fresh information it promises to answer many questions, and perhaps to raise not a few new ones. I commend it to transport enthusiast and industrial historian alike.

J. P. Senior
25 October 1994

Introduction

This book, the result of interests going back over 50 years, is an attempt to produce a useful work of reference for future generations — generations who will not experience smooth and quiet travel by trolleybus. The trolleybus was a form of transport which, with its quick acceleration, was unbeatable by the rival motorbus. The bus was in comparison slow, noisy and carried fewer passengers; indeed, in Huddersfield a 70-seat trolleybus could leave standing a 56-seat bus, despite the fact that the latter made fewer stops per mile.

The trolleybus was a hybrid vehicle which was legally not a light locomotive nor a motor car under the various acts governing road vehicles. This led to difficulties if an offence was committed under the Road Traffic Acts — how to prosecute. Statutory Rules and Orders were issued by the Ministry of Transport after inspection of the relevant 'trackless trolley system' and these defined specific rules for 'trolley vehicles used' on that system.

When Huddersfield Corporation introduced trolleybuses, the corporation was able, due to the legislative muddle, to operate them. The corporation had entered into an agreement in 1929 with the London, Midland & Scottish Railway to operate jointly all bus services. Thus Huddersfield was able solely to operate 'Trackless Trolley Vehicles'.

Many of the early trolleybus routes were feeders to tram routes and, being out of town, often passed relatively unnoticed. As a result, extensive research has been necessary to obtain factual information about pre-1930 trolleybus suppliers and users.

I hope that readers find my interpretation of the trolleybus supply industry to be interesting; I have endeavoured to provide an overview that gives more credit than hitherto to the electrical industry which was, in many cases, the driving force behind vehicle designs as well as the chassis manufacturers.

Geoff Lumb
Huddersfield
February 1995

Half-title page:
In 1928 Nottingham, being unable to purchase two additional double-deck trolleybuses from Railless Ltd, bought two D4 trolleybuses from Ransomes to a very similar specification. The bodies were also built by Ransomes. *GLC*

Title page:
This view of Whitehall Road, Leeds, shows No 501 an RET trolleybus of 1911. The motorist is giving the new trolleybus space to pull out from the kerb. *RET/GLC*

Above:
Manchester placed 38 two-axle postwar trolleybuses of type TDD42/1 into service during 1950 when it converted the Hyde Road to Gee Cross service to trolleybus operation. The batch all had Crossley 8ft-wide bodies. No 1206 is seen waiting until it was time for the conductor to clock in at the roadside clock before continuing its journey. *Author*

Diagrammatic Chart Listing Suppliers

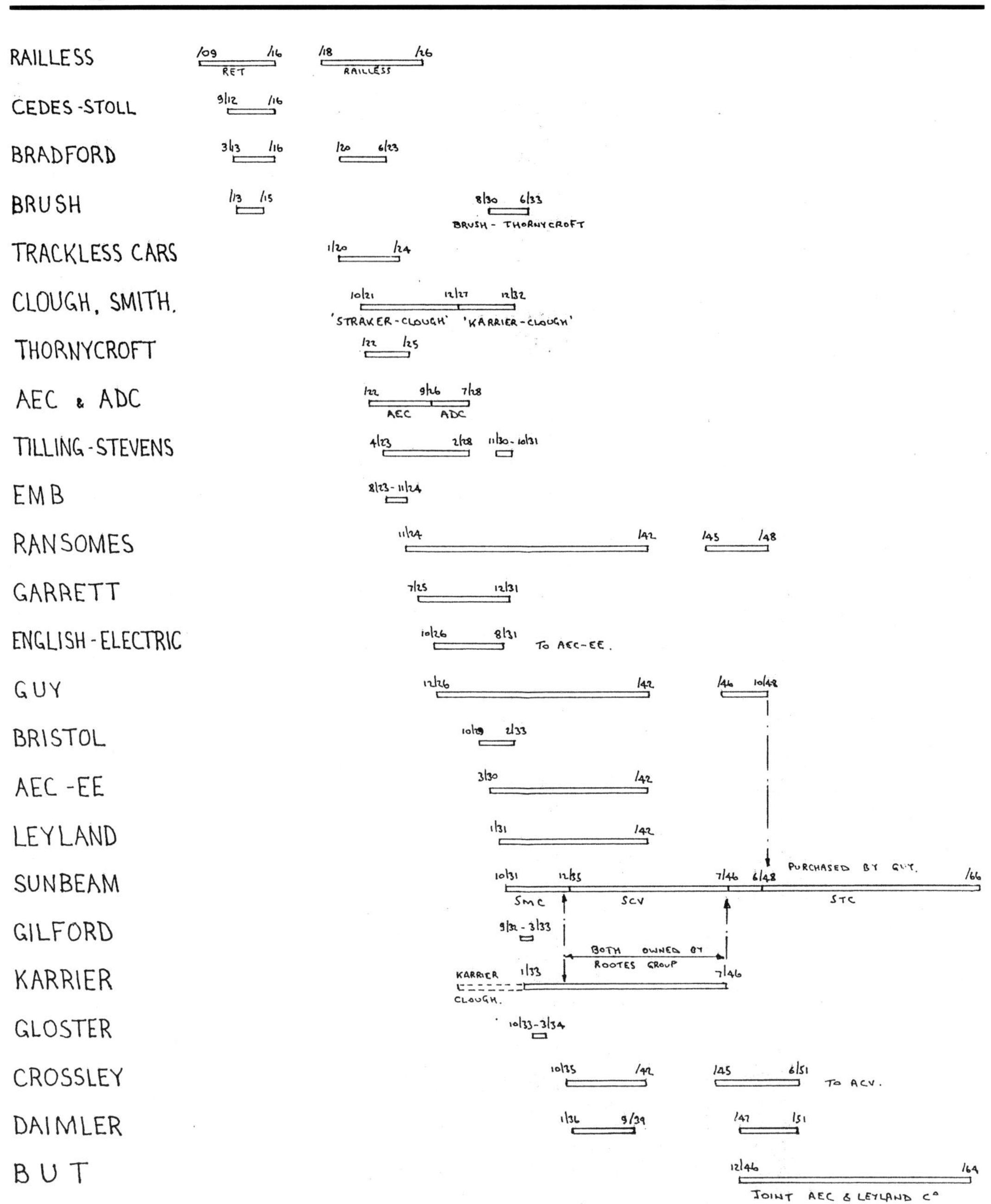

Historical Review

1 Railless to Dennis

In order to put the early suppliers and builders of trolleybuses into perspective it is necessary to understand the circumstances appertaining in the early years of the century.

The tramway mania had waned, many of the tramcar manufacturers were being forced into bankruptcy or into mergers with others and the motorbus was still in its infancy.

The demand for cheap transport without the high costs of installing tramways was met on the continent by the development of the 'Trackless Trolley Tramways' and as early as the spring of 1903 the Halifax Tramways Committee considered the introduction of 'Railless Trams' on three of its routes.

In July 1908 Manchester Corporation sent a deputation to Germany to inspect 'Trackless Trolley Tramways' operated by three local authorities. At the same time a British company The Railless Electric Traction Co Ltd was formed to introduce and develop 'The Trolley Bus' in Britain and other parts of the world. In August 1908 William Martin Murphy, chairman of Dublin United Tramways, advocated introducing electric omnibuses on the 'Trackless Trolley System' between Donnybrook and Bray. Mr Murphy was a shareholder in British Thomson-Houston (BTH) and had held shares in the British Electric Car Co Ltd (BEC) based in Trafford Park, Manchester.

In April 1909 an article in *Motor Traction* on 'Trackless Trolley Systems', giving details of the 'Filovia' system made by the Societa Per La Trazione Electrica, Milan, Italy ended with a statement: 'The sole agency for vehicles on this system in Great Britain has been placed in the hands of a Manchester firm and the cars will be built in England'.

Also in April 1909 negotiations were opened between Trafford Park Estates, Manchester, and the Railless Electric Traction Co of London. The proposals included providing a trolleybus service but nothing came of them. Other residents of the Trafford Park estate included British Westinghouse Electric & Manufacturing Co Ltd, a major competitor of BTH and the United Electric Car Co Ltd of Preston, the current owner of the former British Electric Car Co Ltd (BEC) works.

The same month, April 1909, saw Leeds send three members of a sub-committee — the Chairman, Deputy Chairman and the General Manager of the City Tramways — to the Continent to inspect various systems of Railless Trolley Traction. Their report referred to the English agents for the Max Schiemann system — 'The Railless Electric Traction Co Ltd' — redesigning the German vehicle for British use. In July 1909 the results of these efforts were tested in Birkenhead and then in September 1909 on a test circuit at the Hendon depot of the Metropolitan Electric Tramways Ltd. Contemporary articles said 'It is similar to those at Manchester and is rubber tyred with a chain drive on the rear wheels on either side and two 15ft trolley poles extending from the roof of the driving platform to twin overhead wires. It is at present doubtful whether these cars may be run

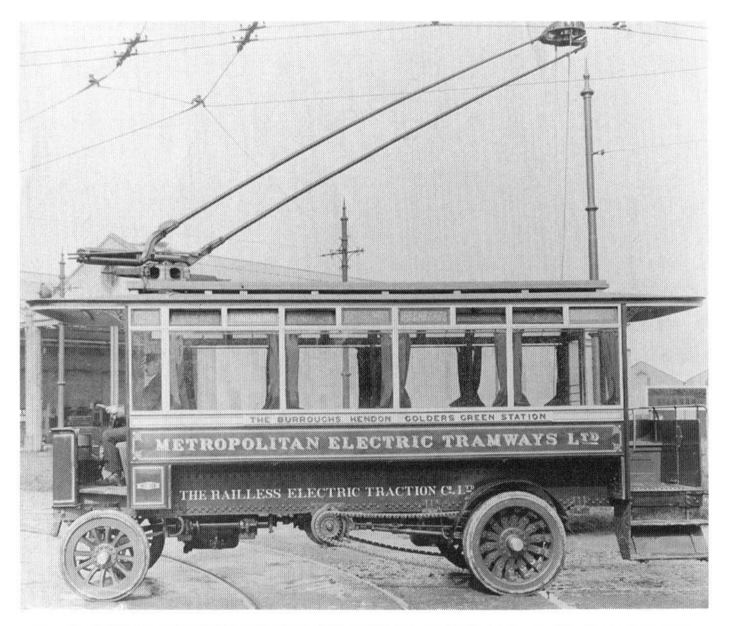

Left:
The first trolleybus in Britain was demonstrated by the Railless Electric Traction Co Ltd at Hendon in September 1909.
RET/Geoff Lumb Collection (GLC)

Above right:
The first trolleybus delivered to Bradford was the Hurst Nelson-bodied Railless Electric Traction vehicle No 240.
Hurst Nelson/GLC

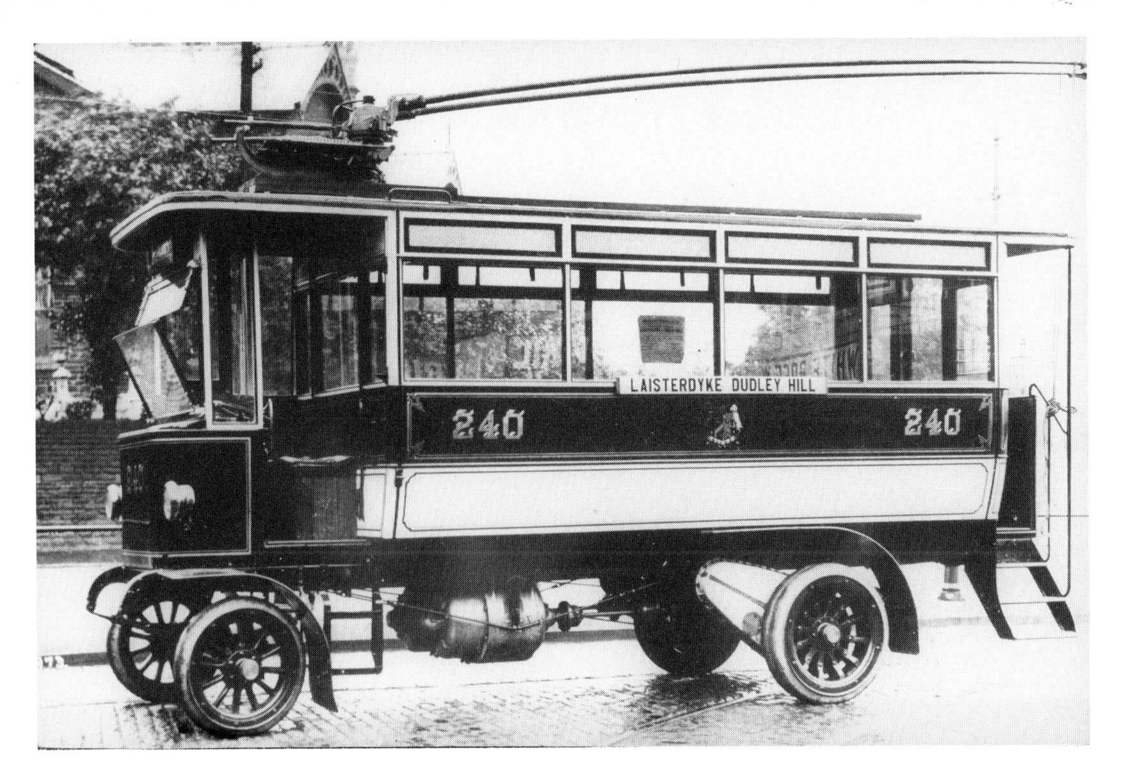

without first obtaining special Parliamentary powers'.

In November 1909, not to be left behind, Bradford sent a delegation of four to the Continent to inspect trackless systems.

During 1910, Cedes Electric Traction Ltd, the British holder of the 'Cedes-Stoll' trackless trolley system, was registered in Britain. Not to be left out in the introduction of trackless trolley systems, the British Electrical Federation in early 1911, after in-depth investigations, arranged for its subsidiary company the Brush Electrical Engineering Co Ltd to obtain and hold the British Licence and patents to produce the trolley omnibus on the Bremen system. In a 1930 Brush catalogue it was said 'The first trolley-buses built in England were built by the Brush Co'.

At this point potential British trolleybus users had the choice of four different systems of current collection:

- The 'RET' system, the British version of the Max Schiemann system, which had two under-running trolley poles with tramcar collector wheels attached to the roof of the trolleybus. The overhead consisted of two wires, one positive and one negative, both being of conventional tramway style 13½in apart.
- 'Cedes-Stoll' system, which had a four-wheeled trolley running on top of the two overhead wires connected to the trackless trolley by a flexible cable which was towed along the route until a trolleybus was met coming in the opposite direction, when it was necessary to unplug the flexible cables from the trolleybuses and exchange them. If desired this could be avoided by erecting two sets of wires.
- 'Bremen' system, which had two wires, the negative one above the positive one. A two-wheeled trolley ran on the top wire and a spring-loaded bow collector slid under the bottom wire. Flexible cables connected the trolley to the trolleybus and again if two trolleybuses needed to pass, it was necessary to exchange the flexible cable and the trolley.
- 'Filovia' system, which used one under-running trolley pole fitted at the outer end with a four-wheel trolley which ran under the two trolley wires. The trolley wires were set 35cm (13¾in) apart. The trolleybus could deviate up to 12ft either side of the overhead against about 15ft deviation for the RET system.

In early 1911 the technical press referred to the orders placed by Leeds and Bradford with Railless Electric Traction Co Ltd for their first trolleybuses with bodies by Hurst Nelson of Motherwell and electrical controllers, equipment and motors by Siemens Bros, Dynamo Works, Stafford.

Bradford is also stated to have placed an order with the United Electric Car Co Ltd of Preston for a 'Filovia'-type trolleybus with UEC body and electrical equipment by Dick, Kerr and Co Ltd. Drawings of this car were also published. On 7 June 1911 'A tower car was run under its own power (petrol

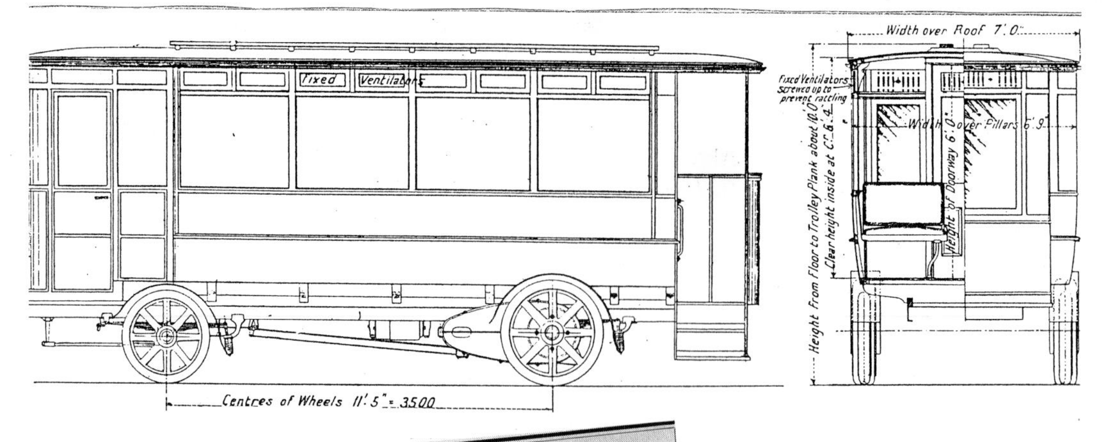

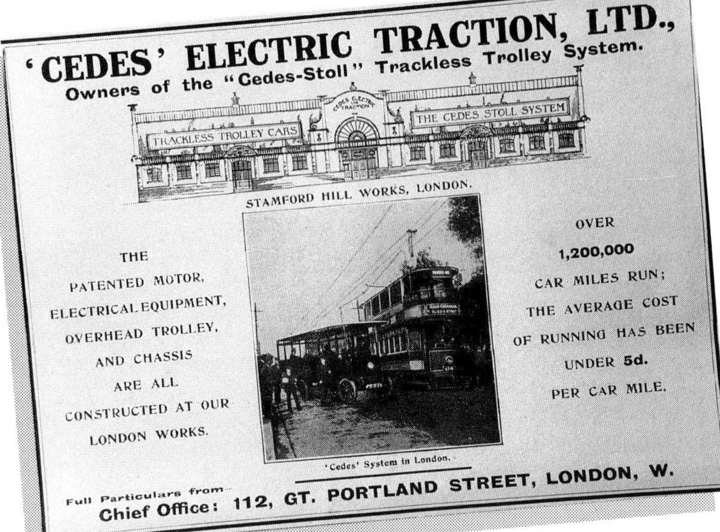

Above:
This drawing of the 'Filovia' car ordered by Bradford Corporation was published in *Tramway and Railway World* in April 1911. *GLC*

Left:
A 1913 'Cedes' Electric Traction advert showing the West Ham demonstration. *GLC*

Right:
Halifax was the only British operator to commence services using second-hand vehicles — two acquired from Dundee. Halifax rebodied one of the duo before services commenced to the highest trolleybus terminus in Britain, Wainstalls (1,027ft above sea level). Rebodied RET No 1 CP2020 is seen at this terminus. *Spencer Wainstalls/GLC*

motors) in order to test how a four-wheel trolley would run on the trolley wires', since the four-wheel trolley was stated earlier to be for the 'Filovia'. For some unexplained reason the 'Filovia' trolley bus did not materialise.

(In parentheses it should be noted that the former works at Trafford Park, Manchester of the British Electric Car Co Ltd was owned by the United Electric Car Co Ltd Preston from 1905 until 1911, when it was taken over by the Ford Motor Co to form their first British car assembly plant. In April 1912 the British agent for the Filovia trackless trolley system was Watlington & Co, London. Dr A. M. Zani, the Milanese inventor of the Filovia system had a brother who worked for Dick, Kerr & Co Ltd at Preston who owned the UEC Co Ltd.)

The 1912 RET brochure reprinted the following quotations from the June 1911 edition of *Electrics*.

'Traction by Wire

'Whether by rail or road, electric traction at its best and cheapest means that power shall be generated at a central economical generating station and transmitted by wire from which the car or train can take such variable quantity as it requires for its purpose.

'The travelling engine driver will be a back number when electric traction becomes more general. Especially on the road must it be economically unsound to carry about a little power station, because there are hills to be encountered and the engine must be sufficiently powerful to climb the incline, which means that it is too powerful for the level. With overhead wires the vehicle helps itself to more power on the slope and less on the level.

'We may safely anticipate therefore, that if road trains have any important future they will not carry engines of any sort but will run on the trolley system.'

Following the introduction of trolleybuses in Leeds

and Bradford in 1911 the scene was set for a further eight systems in the period up to December 1914 plus two experimental lines at Brighton and Hove.

However, when one examines the Parliamentary Bills for all these systems, these either stated that the maximum laden weight of the trolleybuses used had not to exceed five tons or had to have Board of Trade approval.

The original published information on the vehicles supplied to Leeds and Bradford suggests that the unladen weights were about 3ton 12cwt. However, examination of other sources indicates otherwise. In February 1915 'Cedes-Stoll', in response to complaints from Aberdare stated that 'the problems were caused by their 1911 act and the 5-ton limit. The RET at Leeds weighed $4^{3}/_{4}$ton empty and 6ton 3cwt when loaded with 28 passengers and that Leeds disobeyed their act and could be pulled up any time'. Incidentally the Cedes at Keighley weighed 5ton $4^{1}/_{2}$cwt with passengers. At Shanghai during 1916 the unladen weight of the RETs was reduced from $4^{3}/_{4}$ton to $3^{3}/_{4}$ ton by removing one of the two motors and drive.

In a 1914 report prepared by Clough, Smith & Co Ltd on the system in operation in Ramsbottom, the problems incurred by the 5-ton limit were noted 'which, of course, practically means that the vehicle was not to exceed $3^{1}/_{2}$ ton unladen. The chassis and electrical equipment having taken the greater part of this $3^{1}/_{2}$ ton, the car builders were under the necessity of supplying a body which would not weigh more than one ton, and with this object everything was built

Right:
Halifax owned only three trolley-buses, all of which were different. No 2, the 1924 Halifax-bodied Tilling-Stevens, is shown alongside No 103, which was placed in service in 1921 as the spare vehicle after overhaul and repainting. *GLC*

as light as possible and unfortunately, strength had to be sacrificed to attain the object'.

As a result the two Railless trolleybuses at Bradford, which had rear platforms as well, had an unladen weight of 5ton 3cwt. So it is not surprising therefore that Bradford entered into trolleybus design with its Bradford-Browns having an unladen weight of $3\frac{3}{4}$ton, which with 29 passengers would still be overweight but would be over $1\frac{1}{4}$ton lighter than the original Railless cars.

On 4 August 1914 World War 1 started and this immediately caused problems for many of the fledgling users and with the suppliers and builders of trolleybuses.

By September the British Government found it necessary to implement the Trading With The Enemy Act, 1914. This gave the Board of Trade powers, amongst many others, to put companies into receivership if any director was an enemy subject. This meant that the 18 Cedes-Stoll-built vehicles at Aberdare and Keighley and the 12 Brush-built trolleybuses at Stockport, Rhondda and Mexborough & Swinton were all denied spare parts. Guarantees were also all null and void.

The original supplier of motors and control equipment to RET Construction Co Ltd — the German-owned Siemens Bros — was taken over by Dick, Kerr & Co Ltd in 1916 with spares becoming unobtainable since war work took precedence over these. So it is not surprising that in 1916, as it was unable to complete orders for 10 vehicles for North Ormesby, the RET Construction Co Ltd went into receivership. By then the total number of trolleybuses built for the UK was 75 including three demonstrators. A further 35 British-built vehicles are known to have been exported by this date. Clough, Smith & Co Ltd, who were contractors to many of these early systems, found their income of over £17,000 in 1912-13 reduced to £55 in 1917-18.

In April 1918 as the seemingly endless World War 1 dragged on, the Receiver sold the patents and goodwill of the RET Construction Co Ltd to Short Bros (Bedford and Rochester) Ltd, who formed a new company, Railless Ltd, to develop the well-known RET system which had been operating successfully for several years. The new company announced that under the present war conditions, much of the work to be done would be in preparation for the demands which would follow the end of the war and the return of peace when Railless would be the traction of the future.

After the war was over in November 1918, Clough, Smith & Co Ltd were asked by the North Ormesby, South Bank, Normanby & Grangetown Railless Traction Co to clean the overhead they had erected between mid-1915 and early 1916. The 10 trolleybuses, of which four had been reported to be complete

Below:
Wigan was another municipality to operate only three trolleybuses. All were Clough, Smith-supplied Straker-Clough trolley-omnibuses with Brush-built bodies. They had the distinction of being the only trolleybuses in Britain to be fitted in the late 1920s with pneumatic tyres on the front wheels whilst still retaining solid tyres on the rear. *Clough, Smith/GLC*

in 1916, were finished by Railless Ltd and delivered prior to the take-over of the company by the Teesside Railless Traction Board which commenced services in November 1919.

The new services were a success and Clough, Smith & Co Ltd purchased and resold to the TRTB the six Brush-built trolleybuses which had been out of use since early 1915 with the Rhondda Tramways Co (a subsidiary company of the National Electric Construction Co). This purchase enabled the General Manager of the TRTB, Mr J. B. Parker, to compare two different makes and types of vehicle, one being the Railless, with hand-operated controller and two motors one driving each rear wheel, the other being the Brush with a foot-operated controller, a single motor and a motorbus chassis frame.

This led Mr Parker to design a new trolleybus. This would be 'Thoroughly reliable, carry the maximum number of passengers — thought for their comfort being given careful consideration — in fact, a vehicle which could be put on the road and efficiently run, electrically and mechanically, at the lowest possible cost. Several different types of chassis were inspected and examined and the final selection of the Straker-Squire chassis, as used on the London omnibus, was, to my mind, a wise one as the experience this firm has had in designing is of premier importance. The foot-operated controller with one motor has proved itself to be superior to the hand-operated two-motor type, the car driver who has to attend to the ordinary tramway controller and a steering wheel at the same time undoubtedly has both hands full, thus the deletion of the hand-operated controller is certainly an event in railless traction. The inclusion of standard mechanical parts in the omnibus is a salient feature and it was this that originally prompted Mr Parker to put on paper the design that has now materialised as the Straker-Clough Trolley Omnibus,' according to the Chairman of the TRTB, Mr W. G. Grace, on 23 November 1921 in the *Tramway and Railway World*.

At the same time Mr Parker wrote 'The chassis adopted is a standard commercial petrol chassis of noted make (less engine, clutch and gear box), which is fitted up electrically with a single 40hp railway type electric motor, built by an experienced and well-known firm'.

In fact the Straker-Clough trolley-omnibus was marketed by Clough, Smith & Co Ltd, which placed the orders with Straker-Squire for the bare chassis, with BTH for the motor and control equipment and in most cases with the body builders for the body. The only exceptions were the chassis with electrical equipment, supplied to Rotherham, where the user ordered the bodies, and Keighley, which fitted existing bodies to five new chassis.

Meanwhile in November 1920 Bradford had built the first British double-deck trolleybus with a top cover. In October 1921 Leeds introduced the first of three low-height, double-deck railless trolley tractors. These were only 13ft 10in high — nearly 3ft lower than the Bradford one.

Above:
One of the most bizarre trolleybuses built was this one for Rangoon in Burma, which was built on a Ford chassis with BTH traction equipment supplied from Britain. *BTH/GLC*

So the scene was set for the introduction, by other suppliers, of trolleybuses using standard commercial petrol chassis adapted to take electric motors and the high starting torques these imposed on the rear axle. The earlier design using tramway-orientated ideas and equipment lost favour, with Railless Ltd still continuing to use hand controllers and twin motors until 1925.

Many tramway concerns, either municipalities or companies, also had interests in public electric supply services, so the trolleybus was an admirable solution when tramways wore out, as in the case of the Nechells route in Birmingham in 1921, in Keighley in 1924 and also in Ipswich, which after trying Railless and Tilling-Stevens-built trolleybuses supported local manufacturers Ransomes, Sims & Jefferies Ltd and Garrett Ltd for its large orders.

The next important development in trolleybus design was the introduction of low-loading models. Then in December 1926 Guy Motors Ltd of Wolverhampton built its first trolleybus, which was also the first three-axle double-deck trolleybus on pneumatic tyres. This was to set the trend for the next decade.

By early 1927 the speed limit was still 12mph, whilst the number of trolleybuses operating over 87.04 route miles by the 20 trolleybus undertakings was 258.

During 1925 Clough, Smith & Co Ltd found itself in difficulties when the company chassis supplier Straker-Squire went into receivership causing problems with orders already placed. By 1927 Clough, Smith & Co had made arrangements to use chassis supplied by Karrier Motors Ltd, Huddersfield, as the basis for the new 'Karrier-Clough Trolley Omnibus', which Clough, Smith & Co marketed.

Meanwhile in 1926 Short Bros (Bedford and Rochester) Ltd, the parent company of Railless Ltd, had ceased to manufacture Railless trolleybuses to enable them to concentrate on more profitable activities in bodybuilding and aircraft production. This encouraged the English Electric Co Ltd, which had previously supplied all the motors and electrical equipment for all the trolleybuses built by Railless Ltd, to provide chassis also. The English Electric Co Ltd did not want to lose their share of the market and purchased a Leyland chassis less engine, clutch and gear box as the basis for their first step towards supplying complete trolleybuses.

After the initial Leyland based chassis, English Electric produced its own chassis for single and double-deck vehicles. Unfortunately the foot-operated controller used was not the most successful and early English Electric products earned the nickname 'Paddlers'. Additional minor design faults caused other problems. Moreover, the company was having financial difficulties with the result that in 1930 a new Managing Director, Mr G. H. Nelson, was appointed to get the company back on to its feet with quality products. In February, the company was reorganised and in March 1930 a joint venture was launched with AEC Ltd. The latter company would provide trolleybus chassis with English Electric motors and equipment and initially with English Electric building the body.

This was also the turning point for AEC since the company built only 14 trolleybuses, including ADC marketed ones, for British operators since 1922.

During the early 1930s, the general trade depression hit the motor manufacturing industry and Bristol, Brush-Thornycroft and Sunbeam-BTH all began offering trolleybuses using unsold six-wheeled motorbus chassis as the base.

In 1932 Clough, Smith & Co Ltd ceased to market

the 'Karrier-Clough Trolley Omnibus' but continued to design and install overhead and power supplies to many trolleybus conversions and extensions. At this point Karrier Motors Ltd began marketing trolleybuses as the company's own product until they were taken over by Humber Ltd in 1934.

Also in 1932 Leyland Motors Ltd, anxious not to be left out of the rapidly expanding market for trolleybuses, linked forces with General Electric Co Ltd, Witton, Birmingham to produce the Leyland-GEC trolleybus.

Both Gilford Motor Co Ltd, who joined forces with Electric Construction Co Ltd, and Gloucester Railway Carriage & Wagon Co Ltd tried unsuccessfully to enter the market, each one just producing a single trolleybus. In 1935 Crossley Motors Ltd began to produce and supply trolleybuses for the potential needs of Manchester and Ashton-under-Lyne corporations, who were expected to convert tram routes to trolleybus operation shortly. Both were already important users of Crossley motorbuses.

The last of the new manufacturers to emerge, in 1936, was Transport Vehicles (Daimler) Ltd which, also to protect its interests, started producing four and six-wheel Daimler trolleybuses. To encourage Daimler motorbus users to use Daimler trolleybuses when their tramways were converted to trolleybus operation, the company provided demonstrators 'free of charge' for months.

By 1936 many potential users wanting to use local products, in order to encourage local industry and suppliers and to create jobs for local residents and

Left:
The final solution for many trolleybus operators was to purchase second-hand trolleybuses and rebody others. This scene at Teesside shows examples of both.
Ian Allan Library

ratepayers, forced the chassis manufacturers to offer alternative electrical equipment, eg:

- Leyland used Metropolitan-Vickers equipment for Manchester, Ashton and South Lancashire.
- AEC used Crompton-Parkinson/Allan West equipment for Brighton.

In 1935 Humber Ltd (Rootes Securities), who had also just purchased Sunbeam Commercial Vehicles Ltd, transferred the production of Karrier trolleybuses to the Sunbeam factory in Wolverhampton and then in December 1935 AEC Ltd took a financial interest in Sunbeam with two AEC directors on the Board.

In 1937 the demand for the British trolleybus reached a peak and 24 examples, some in chassis form and some with bodies, were displayed by 14 chassis and body suppliers at the 1937 Commercial Motor Show.

When World War 2 started in September 1939, there were still eight chassis suppliers in business. Some of these were immediately compelled to cease production to concentrate on war work, some orders were cancelled or transferred to other suppliers and some overseas orders were diverted to the home market.

With large numbers of elderly trolleybuses still in service the growing need for replacements was met by the Ministry of War Transport which arranged for the Wolverhampton factory of Sunbeam to produce two-axle chassis, for either single or double-deck bodies, for sale by Sunbeam or Karrier Motors Ltd. The Sunbeam ones were sold by Sunbeam Commercial Vehicles Ltd, Wolverhampton, and the Karrier ones were sold by Karrier Motors Ltd, Biscot Road, Luton, the plates and badges stating the appropriate sales organisation. Where MoWT trolleybuses were bought it was often on the condition that replaced vehicles were sold to operators who did not qualify for new vehicles. This led to unreliable and troublesome vehicles being sold first, eg Bradford ones to Newcastle and South Shields.

Some operators would not accept two-axle trolleybuses and placed orders during the war for three-axle trolleybuses to be supplied as soon as circumstances allowed, often having to wait years for delivery. For example, Huddersfield's Karrier MS2 vehicles, which were ordered in 1945, were delivered between July 1947 and July 1948, allowing 12 displaced elderly trolleybuses to be sold to Reading.

In July 1946, after AEC had disposed of their interests in Sunbeam, Humber Ltd sold its Sunbeam factory to Brockhouse & Co, at the same time retaining the Karrier Motors Co Ltd name for its own use. This meant that all outstanding orders for Karrier trolleybuses, placed before the July 1946 sale, were completed as Karrier but no orders for Karrier trolleybuses could be accepted after that date. So identical vehicles at Huddersfield either carried Karrier or Sunbeam badges depending on the date on which the order had been placed. In Ipswich the last Karrier F4 to enter service did not do so until January 1949.

In June 1948 Brockhouse renamed the Sunbeam company as 'The Sunbeam Trolleybus Co Ltd' and then in October 1948 resold the business and factory to Guy Motors Ltd who then ceased to build its own Guy range of trolleybuses but continued to develop the Sunbeam business instead.

Meanwhile in December 1946 a new company, British United Traction Ltd, had been formed to handle the trolleybus activities of the two parent companies AEC and Leyland, initially transferring production to the old Leyland factory at Kingston-upon-Thames but leaving some production at Southall and Leyland. After Crossley were taken over by ACV Ltd, production of double-deck BUTs was moved to Crossley's Stockport works and the last single-deck BUTs were assembled in the Scammell works at Watford.

The nationalisation of the electricity supply industry in 1947/48 forced many operators to pay more for electric power and, after the initial backlog of postwar orders was completed, the trolleybus industry went into steady decline with Crossley, Daimler, Guy and Ransomes all ceasing to make

Above:
The only time South Yorkshire PTE allowed fare-paying passengers to travel on its Dennis Dominator demonstration trolleybus over the one-mile-long test route in Doncaster was on 8 September 1985. *David Smithies*

trolleybuses by 1951. This left just BUT and Sunbeam to carry on until 1962, when Sunbeam supplied the last batch of trolleybuses to a British operator, Bournemouth, followed by their last batch of six similar chassis, which entered service in Coimbra, Portugal, in 1966. The last BUTs were built at the Scammell factory, Watford, in 1964 for use in Wellington, New Zealand.

With the gradual decline of British operators many vehicles were resold for further use whilst many others were refurbished and fitted with new bodies to prolong their lifetime. So despite receiving its last new vehicle in January 1951, Bradford continued, by careful management, to operate trolleybuses until March 1972. Bradford was the last British operator to operate trolleybuses commercially as well as being one of the first to operate them in 1911, over 60 years earlier.

In 1974 the municipalities in the West Riding of Yorkshire were taken over by two Passenger Transport Executives (PTEs). Both the West Yorkshire PTE, which included Leeds and Bradford in its area, and the South Yorkshire PTE, which included Doncaster and Rotherham, have put forward various schemes for reintroducing trolleybuses in their areas. So far Government funding has not been forthcoming and with the deregulation of local bus services in 1985 these plans may never be viable without financial protection for the operator.

However, in 1984 South Yorkshire PTE sponsored the building of an experimental chopper-controlled trolleybus. The chassis used was built by Hestair Dennis Ltd who adapted a standard Dominator double-deck chassis, fitting a 132kW traction motor supplied by GEC Traction Ltd. This was controlled by a modern thyristor (chopper) equipment package, an auxiliary type 3DA Dorman Diesel engine being fitted for manoeuvring away from traction wires. The diesel engine, after allowing for other electrical loads such as lighting, power and steering, supplied 29kW for traction purposes. The vehicle was designed for a top road speed of 40mph and was fitted with a standard double-deck body built by Alexanders.

In August 1985 it was tested on private roads at Doncaster Racecourse and performance proved to be satisfactory. When the project was put on hold the vehicle was moved to the trolleybus museum at Sandtoft for display purposes.

In the 1990s, although the trolleybus may have disappeared from the nation's streets, one can still see and travel on British-built trolleybuses at various preservation sites in Britain. These include Sandtoft, Carlton Colville and the Black Country Museum at Dudley.

The Manufacturers

2 AEC/ADC

Associated Equipment Co Ltd
Associated Daimler Co Ltd

The introduction in early 1922 of a railless trolley-omnibus by the Associated Equipment Co Ltd of Walthamstow, London, was an important milestone in trolleybus development. It was the first attempt by a petrol chassis manufacturer to enter the market for electric trolley-omnibuses, previous vehicles having been built by people whose experience was biased to tramway engineering practice. The AEC chassis was designed with construction kept simple for maintenance and used a single 33.5bhp, BTH motor with rheostatic control.

Six examples of this first model 602 were built; three went to the Mexborough & Swinton Tramways Co and two were built for use as sale or return demonstrators for Leeds and Birmingham during the summer of 1923. These latter two were both bought by Leeds City Tramways in December 1923. The final 602 chassis was sold by Maj Madson, the AEC agent in Melbourne, Australia in July 1923 to Inglis Bros, New Zealand, who had it bodied by DSC & Cousins, Auckland, before it entered service with Wellington Corporation Tramways on a route less than a mile long, from Thorndon to Kaiwarra, in September 1924 to become Australasia's first trolley-omnibus.

Also in early 1922 a prototype chassis was built for Shanghai Electric Construction Co. This was designated model 603 and it led to an order being received in late 1924 for 100 chassis and trailers. The main feature of this design was a set-back front axle to allow for a forward front entrance. A Bull motor and EMB controller were fitted. One of these chassis with trailer was tested at Ipswich in June 1925. Over 220 examples of this type were built for Shanghai and its associated company in Singapore in the period up to 1930.

The next development, in September 1925, was a prototype short wheelbase trolleybus with one-man-operated, 30 seat, Strachan & Brown body. Although the technical press called it a new improved model 603, it was actually an 'XU' chassis Number U 78, with a wheelbase of 10ft 8$^{3}/_{4}$in and was fitted with a 50hp Bull motor and EMB foot-operated controller. It was registered by Leeds for its first demonstration before moving to Bradford in October 1925. After further demonstrations at Oldham in May 1926, Ashton in June 1926 and Manchester in July 1927, it arrived in Southend for trials in September 1927 and was purchased by Southend Corporation in March 1928.

Meanwhile in early 1926, AEC built its only model 607 double-deck trolleybus with a wheelbase of 15ft 9in. It was fitted with a Bull 55hp motor and a 52 seat rear open staircase body built by Vickers. After use as

Left:
AEC built its first trolleybus Type 602 in 1922. It is seen here on test at Manvers Main on the Mexborough & Swinton system.
Ian Allan Library

a demonstrator it was sold to Birmingham Corporation in 1926.

In June 1926 AEC Ltd and Daimler Co Ltd joined forces to market both companies' products under the name of Associated Daimler Co Ltd which they continued to do until July 1928.

The first trolleybuses delivered under the ADC banner were four model 607 chassis fitted with centre entrance, Strachan & Brown 36-seat, single-deck bodies. This time the front axle was set back to give a wheelbase of 14ft 6in. Three entered service in August/September 1926 at Bradford and the other one was exhibited at the Municipal Tramways Association Conference in Liverpool before eventual sale to Bradford in December 1926.

After the successful trials with the prototype 'XU' trolleybus, ADC introduced the 604 having left-hand drive and 605 having conventional right-hand drive. The only sales for the 604, were two for Gemeente Trams, Groningen, Holland, with Vickers 24-seat bodies, in May 1927, and a repeat order for four more in July 1928.

Bradford was the only purchaser of the 605, having three with 30-seat Strachan & Brown bodies. The 605 had a wheelbase of 13ft 6in and had Bull 50hp motors.

The dimensions of these 604 and 605 models as built differed from specifications published in the period 1925 to 1927. Hence Bradford actually ordered model 603s but received 605s.

The technical press when reviewing the AEC 607 double-deck in early 1926 commented that 'manufacturers of trolley-omnibuses are beginning to realise that this form of traction presents problems peculiar to itself and that a petrol chassis converted or modified to take an electric motor instead of an internal combustion engine is not the best foundation on which to build up an efficient trolley omnibus.'

AEC had moved production from Walthamstow to Southall in early 1927, and after the break-up with Daimler in July 1928, no further orders were received for home use. With the appointment in July 1928 of a new Chief Engineer, Mr G. J. Rackman, AEC concentrated on developing more durable products which were built from 1929.

At the same time the English Electric Co Ltd was having difficulties in producing a durable and reliable trolleybus, so in March 1930 AEC and EE joined forces to produce jointly rather than each trying to solve problems beyond their immediate experience.

Below:
One of the two AEC Type 602 demonstration trolleybuses purchased by Leeds in 1923. It is seen inside the depot at Guiseley and was used on the services to Otley and Burley from White Cross, Guiseley. *GLC*

Above right:
The demonstrator AEC Type XU trolleybus, an improved Type 603 built in 1925, was fitted with a Strachan & Brown front-entrance body before testing and demonstration on a number of systems. *AEC/GLC*

Below right:
Birmingham purchased in 1926 the only AEC double-deck Type 607 trolleybus built. It was fitted with a rear open staircase body built by Vickers at Crayford. *AEC/GLC*

BEWARE
OF
MOVING
TRUCKS
AEC
SPEED 12 M.P.H

518

Above:
One of four Type 607 trolleybuses built by AEC and sold by the Associated Daimler Co Ltd was this example used by ADC as a demonstrator before joining the other three in service with Bradford in late 1926. *AEC/GLC*

Left:
In 1927 two ADC Type 604 left-hand-drive trolleybuses were built and fitted with Vickers 24-seat bodies for export to Gemeente Trams, Groningen, in the Netherlands. *Ian Allan Library*

Below left:
This is one of three Type 605 one-man-operated trolleybuses built in 1927 for Bradford Corporation. The trio were fitted with Strachan & Brown 30-seat bodies. *Strachan & Brown/GLC*

3 AEC/EEC

Associated Equipment Co Ltd, Southall English Electric Co Ltd, Traction Dept, Bradford

After the agreement in March 1930 between AEC Ltd and English Electric Co Ltd, it was announced in April 1930 that three models would be produced, AEC manufacturing the chassis and components and the English Electric Co the electrical equipment and bodies. The three models were as follows:

- 661T — two-axle, 15ft 6½in wheelbase for 50/52-seat double-deck body.
- 662T — two-axle, 17ft 0in wheelbase for 30/34-seat single-deck body.
- 663T — three-axle, 16ft 6in wheelbase for 60-seat double-deck body. (The 663T was also offered with an 18ft 7in wheelbase.)

In these first models the single electric motor was mounted forward in a similar position to that of a petrol engine. They were distinguished by their relatively light weight and low loading height. For those cases where a motor mounted in a forward position was not favoured, the complete English Electric vehicle, in which the motor of either single or double type was mounted in the middle of the chassis frame, could still be supplied. Hence orders were still received for pure English Electric vehicles.

In May 1930 the first 3 prototype vehicles were being built with EEC bodies, 13ft 8⁹⁄₁₆in high, seating 27 in the lower saloon and 33 in the upper saloon, on AEC chassis numbers 663T, 001-3. The first one was completed in June for demonstration purposes at the same time as the first order was received from Walsall Corporation for two 663Ts. These were the first two to be constructed by EEC where the body shell was built as a single unit and not as two separate saloons.

It seems that the full-fronted design of these early AEC-EEC trolleybuses made access to the forward-mounted motors difficult as well as having body defects. At least two of the three prototypes had new EEC bodies built for them incorporating a half cab

Below:
One of the three prototype AEC/EE Type 663T trolleybuses built in 1930 with English Electric 60-seat bodies of five-bay layout, which, due to structural problems, had to receive replacement six-bay bodies. This is not the vehicle that was tested at the Fulwell depot of London United in 1930 before going for demonstration to the South Lancashire system as fleet No 11. *EE/GLC*

Above:
In 1931 London United introduced 60 AEC Type 663T trolleybuses with 56-seat bodies built by the Union Construction Co Ltd of Feltham. These were the first trolleybuses built with half-cabs and bonnets, hence the nickname 'Diddlers'. The rear platform gave access to the straight offside staircase. *GLC*

Left:
One of the three prototype AEC/EE Type 663T trolleybuses was rebuilt in 1931 with a new half cab English Electric body. It was shown at the 1931 Commercial Motor Show before being demonstrated at Bradford and elsewhere before being sold to Southend (as No 116) in 1932. *EE/GLC*

design with dummy radiator so resembling contemporary AEC motorbuses. The third chassis 663T-002, was updated and reworked as 663T-070, and fitted with a new Short Bros body for sale to Birmingham in 1932.

Production orders for 661T, 662T and 663T were fitted with this style of half cab until 1932 with EEC not always being the automatic choice for electrical equipment or body builder, eg BTH motors were used on 25 of the 60 London United 'Diddlers'.

In 1932 a new design of specialised trolleybus was announced by AEC. These included the only 691T, three-axle trolleybus built for London United as fleet No 61, the 761T, two-axle trolleybuses based on the AEC 'Q' side-engined motorbuses, followed by a range of 661T, 662T, 663T, and 664T models with motors mounted amidships within the chassis frame. Again electrical equipment was not always supplied by EE, although both companies still promoted the joint venture.

The total number of AEC trolleybuses produced in this period were:

661T	1931-41	number built	380
662T	1932-37	number built	28
663T	1930-39	number built	89
691T	1933	number built	1
761T	1933-34	number built	5
664T	1935-42	number built	844
		Grand Total	1347

These included parts used for three experimental, chassisless vehicles for the London Passenger Transport Board — Class X4 (No 754), pre-production Class M1 (No 953) and pre-production Class L2 (No 954) — as well as the 25 production Class M1. In addition, AEC supplied 176 sets of parts and axles for LPTB classes L1, L2, L3 and X5. As a result of these orders, AEC was the most successful supplier in the 1930s. For production after 1946 see BUT.

Above:
This close-up of a 1932 AEC/EE Type 662T trolleybus for Notts & Derby Traction Co shows the traction control equipment housed under the bonnet behind the false radiator. *EE/GLC*

Above right:
In 1933 Notts & Derby purchased 15 more AEC/EE Type 661T trolleybuses with Metro-Cammell-Weymann bodies. *GLC*

Below:
In early 1933 AEC built an experimental chassis, Type 691T. It was fitted with a 74-seat London General-built body 30ft in length. The central entrance was fitted with double sliding pneumatically-operated doors. It was placed in service in March 1933 on the LUT routes at Kingston-upon-Thames as fleet No 61. In the week commencing 12 June 1933 it was demonstrated at Bournemouth for the benefit of the delegates to the Electrical Convention. It could thus be compared to the recently delivered AEC Type 663T trolleybus which Bournemouth Corporation had hired for its trial route. *AEC/GLC*

Above:
In October 1933 AEC/EE built and displayed a new experimental trolleybus chassis, the 761T, at the Olympia Show. The English Electric-built body had a forward entrance and could seat 63 passengers. After testing on the Bradford system it was purchased by Bradford Corporation in February 1934. The vehicle was a trolleybus version of the AEC 'Q' type motorbus and only five were built. Southend purchased the only other UK-operated example, the remaining three being supplied to Sydney, Australia. *EE/GLC*

Above:
Huddersfield's one and only AEC/EE Type 663T trolleybus was fitted with a 60-seat English Electric body and was purchased in late 1933 for evaluation with vehicles from Ransomes, Sunbeam and Karrier. *AEC/GLC*

Below:
The only long wheelbase Type 663T trolleybus built by AEC was supplied to London Transport (LPTB) in 1934 as fleet No 62. This vehicle was effectively the prototype for many hundreds of later vehicles which were built with 30ft-long bodies. *Ian Allan Library*

Above:
In 1936 Grimsby placed 10 AEC/EE Type 663T trolleybuses in service. These were fitted with attractive 58-seat centre-entrance bodies built by C. H. Roe. *Roe/GLC*

Right:
Bradford No 605, a 1934 AEC/EE Type 661T, was the first one to be rebodied in 1944 with a Brush Coachworks 58-seat body. *Brush/GLC*

Left:
Bradford No 670 was one of the last AEC/EE Type 661Ts to be bought new in 1938. It carried a standard metal-framed English Electric body. *EE/GLC*

Centre left:
Darlington was the only UK customer for the AEC Type 662T single-deck trolleybus with full-width cab. Despite this improvement, the style of bodywork was archaic when built in 1934 by English Electric (Dick, Kerr coachwork). Compare it with the other UK 662T user, Notts & Derby, an example of which was illustrated earlier. *EE/GLC*

Below:
Only two UK trolleybus undertakings purchased AEC Type 661T trolleybuses fitted with Park Royal 56-seat bodies. This view of Cleethorpes No 50 shows its neat lines and the low unladen weight of 6ton 13cwt 1qr. *Dave Hurley/GLC*

Right:
Various operators chose Weymann to build elegant bodies for their AEC 661T trolleybuses. Brighton Corporation No 3 is similar to ones supplied to Notts & Derby and Hastings Tramways, as well as the eight supplied to Brighton & Hove in 1939 (which did not enter service until 1946). The last Type 661Ts built were the 10 supplied in 1941/42 to Notts & Derby.
Dave Hurley/GLC

Centre right:
The first customer for the 30ft-long AEC Type 664T was Newcastle, which, in 1935, placed 10 AEC/EE examples in service. Five, like this one, had English Electric-built bodies; the remaining five had Brush-supplied bodies. All 10 seated 60, dual staircases allowing for rear entrance/front exit passenger flow. *EE/GLC*

Below:
In 1937 AEC/EE supplied two Type 664T trolleybuses to Moscow with left-hand drive. The English Electric-built bodies were 8ft wide and are believed to have been 33ft long. The single-deck example had seating for only 33 and was intended to carry a significant number of standing passengers as well. *EE/GLC*

Left:
The double-deck example supplied to Moscow in 1937 illustrates the 8ft-wide body overhanging the standard 7ft 6in-width axles. *EE/GLC*

Right:
In 1937 London Transport built a prototype chassisless trolleybus at its Charlton Works. This incorporated AEC 664T running units. No 754 was built with a front exit and seated 68 passengers. *EE/GLC*

Left:
Also in 1937 AEC/EE built seven special 664T trolleybuses with the front axle set back to allow a forward-entrance MCCW body to be fitted. The vehicles were destined for Montreal Transport in Canada. *AEC/GLC*

Right:
Only 50 of London Transport's trolleybuses had bodies built by Park Royal. No 1645 was one of the 25 built in 1939. It was an AEC 664T chassis fitted with a 70-seat body.
Dave Hurley/GLC

Left:
In 1940 English Electric built and bodied a prototype chassisless trolleybus incorporating AEC 664T running units. *EE/GLC*

Right:
The last AEC Type 664T trolleybuses built were the 10 supplied for Cardiff's first trolleybus route in 1941. These were fitted with Northern Counties bodies built in Wigan. Northern Counties was owned by the Hall Lewis family who also had considerable business interests in Cardiff. The chassis order had been placed with Leyland Motors but, due to war work, it was transferred to AEC.
EE/GLC

4 Bradford-Brown

The Bradford City Tramways manager Mr C. J. Spencer was dissatisfied with the two 1911 Railless Electric Traction Co-built trolleybuses which were constantly giving trouble due to the roads they had to run on. These roads were either laid with granite setts or were roughly laid with waterbound limestone macadam, the surface of which was often potholed and rutted. The electrical equipment, more suitable for use on tramways with steel rails, obviously suffered from constant vibration and clouds of dust from the poor road surfaces. In addition, the poor road surfaces meant that the suspension, transmission and chain drive were severely strained. The fact that parts of the vehicle had been made as light as possible to comply with the 1910 Act did not help and yet these vehicles still had an unladen weight of 5ton 3cwt which meant that when laden they actually weighed over $6\frac{1}{2}$ton.

In an effort to solve these problems C. J. Spencer and J. W. Dawson, the tramway engineer, designed in late 1912 a Railless Electric Vehicle (REV) which was 'much lighter and sweeter running'. Drawings were produced for a 12ft 9in wheelbase chassis with frames made from $\frac{3}{16}$in thick steel formed and pressed to shape, a Kirkstall Forge front axle, two Siemens 20hp motors each driving a rear wheel through two worm-driven units in the rear axle so avoiding the earlier chain drive problems. Where possible standard parts from the Dodson Car already being produced by David Brown & Sons Ltd, Huddersfield, were used. The chassis was assembled by David Brown's with a 29-seat teak framed body being built at Bradford's Thornbury Works. The vehicle was completed before the end of March 1913. In December 1913, impressed with this first Bradford-Brown REV, the unladen weight of which was $3\frac{3}{4}$ton, tenders were invited by the Council, which sanctioned in January 1914 the construction of a further 28 REVs. From these parts, Bradford completed 17 trolleybuses, 15 between June and December 1914 and the last two in April 1915.

With the outbreak of war in August 1914, Bradford invited offers for the last 10 sets of parts and on 28 September 1914, after the highest tenderer had withdrawn, 10 chassis were sold to Leeds City Tramways. Leeds used five chassis and built 14 bodies for them at their Kirkstall Road Works, enabling Leeds to commence operation of the Guiseley-Otley/Burley services introduced in September and October 1915. After RET Construction went into receivership in 1916, it

Below:
The first of 18 trolleybuses to be built at Bradford Corporation's Thornbury Works using David Brown chassis frames, No 503 was built in 1913. The 29-seat body was built by Thornbury. *GLC*

Right:
No 505 was the first of five trolley-buses completed by Leeds Corporation at its Kirkstall Works using Bradford-Brown chassis. This vehicle was used to open new routes from Guiseley to Otley in September 1915. *GLC*

appears that Leeds used some of the Bradford-Brown parts and spare bodies to rebuild three of the original four 1911 RETs. In the 1923 Board of Trade returns, Leeds had only trolleybuses of its own manufacture in service! What is not clear is what happened to the 28th chassis.

By July 1916, Bradford found it necessary to fit tie bars to stiffen up its lighter chassis, increasing the unladen weight to 3ton, 19cwt and 2qr.

In October 1918 a new manager Mr R. H. Wilkinson was appointed. He continued to develop the trolleybus system and in November 1920 the first double-deck trolleybus with a top cover was completed by the Thornbury Works. This was followed by a twin steer, double-deck trolleybus in January 1922.

Bradford's last home products were six, 30-seat single-deckers built between December 1922 and June 1923. After this Bradford purchased its trolley-buses from the up and coming suppliers.

Above:
In 1920 Bradford Corporation built trolleybus No 521 using a Kirkstall Forge chassis. The Thornbury-built body made No 521 the first double-deck trolleybus to be fitted with a top cover. *BCT/GLC*

Right:
In 1922 Bradford built its second double-deck trolleybus No 522. In order to make control of the vehicle easier for the driver, twin steering axles were fitted at the front to reduce the effort needed to steer it. Only one other trolleybus was to use twin steering axles; this was the Leyland experimental vehicle of 1939. *GLC*

Left:
This rear view of Bradford No 522 shows clearly the tramway influence in contemporary trolleybus design. *GLC*

Below:
In December 1922 Bradford placed in service No 523. This was the first of a batch of six trolleybuses which were to be the last built at Thornbury. Again Kirkstall Forge chassis components were used. The vehicles were fitted with Thornbury-built bodies seating 30 and were designed for one-man operation. *Keighley News/GLC*

5 Bristol

Above:
The second Bristol trolleybus was built in 1931 as a demonstrator. It was fitted with a Beadle 60-seat body. After testing on the Pontypridd system it was purchased by that UDC as fleet No 9.
C. Taylor Collection

In 1929 the Bristol Tramways & Carriage Co Ltd, Tramways Centre, Bristol (as a highly successful manufacturer of motorbuses), was encouraged by one of its many municipal customers, Doncaster Corporation, to offer its 6W PSV chassis with an electric motor instead of a petrol engine. Both types of chassis were shown at the 1929 Commercial Motor Show.

The trolleybus chassis had many features similar to the contemporary Karrier-Clough trolleybuses in service at Doncaster, including spectacle frame and a BTH 60hp motor and equipment.

Bristol Tramways & Carriage Co placed an order for the trolleybus chassis E101 to have a 60-seat body built by C. H. Roe in Leeds to its general order number 1598. The Roe records show that the body was built by Thornton and Houson, two of its craftsmen, and was completed on 21 August 1930. It was not lettered but carried registration number DT2620 when it left Roe.

Doncaster Corporation records show that it arrived for extended trials in August 1930 and ran on loan to them until 11 February 1932, when it was purchased and given fleet number 31. In appearance it was similar to the other Doncaster 1930 Karrier-Clough trolleybuses Nos 17-23, although the seating layout was slightly different.

The only other Bristol trolleybus chassis No E102 was constructed in 1930 by converting motorbus chassis No C101. This was fitted with a 60-seat body built by Beadle. It was then tested inside Brislington tram depot and possibly in Victoria Street in Bristol. It was registered as HY2391 and was demonstrated to another Bristol user, Pontypridd UDC in 1931. In 1932 it was given fleet No 9 by the UDC after purchase. This one was fitted with a Bull motor.

6 Brush

Brush-Lloyd-Kohler

Brush-Thornycroft

The Brush Electrical Engineering Co Ltd at Loughborough held the British licence to produce trolleybuses on the Lloyd-Kohler or Bremen system. Publicity material issued by the company in 1922 and 1930 claimed that they had built the first trolleybuses in England in 1911.

In 1913 they built three trolleybuses for Stockport Corporation, Brush adapting and fitting electrical equipment and a single 35hp interpole motor with shaft drive to an overhead worm rear axle in a basic 3-4ton CC model chassis purchased from the Daimler Motor Co Ltd, Coventry. This chassis, designed by Frank Searle in 1912, after he left AEC, was being purchased by the British Electric Traction group for its subsidiary companies which were commencing operation of motorbuses, naturally using its subsidiary company Brush to build the bodies.

These were the first British trolleybuses to use a pedal-control system instead of a tram-type hand controller, leaving both the driver's hands free for steering purposes. The drum for the Lloyd-Kohler current collector cable was housed under the front scuttle.

The next orders to be received were from the National Electric Construction Co Ltd — six for Rhondda Tramways Co Ltd and three for Mexborough & Swinton Tramways Co Ltd, both being NEC subsidiary companies. Both wished to use the Trackless cars along tramways with a trailing skate and existing tramway overhead to gain access to intended routes. Brush was persuaded to fit under-running trolleys instead of the orthodox Lloyd-Kohler system. In order to avoid infringing the RET patents of current collection Brush fitted two trolleys, one mounted vertically above the other, to become the first known application of this type in Britain, which had been patented by Estler in 1912.

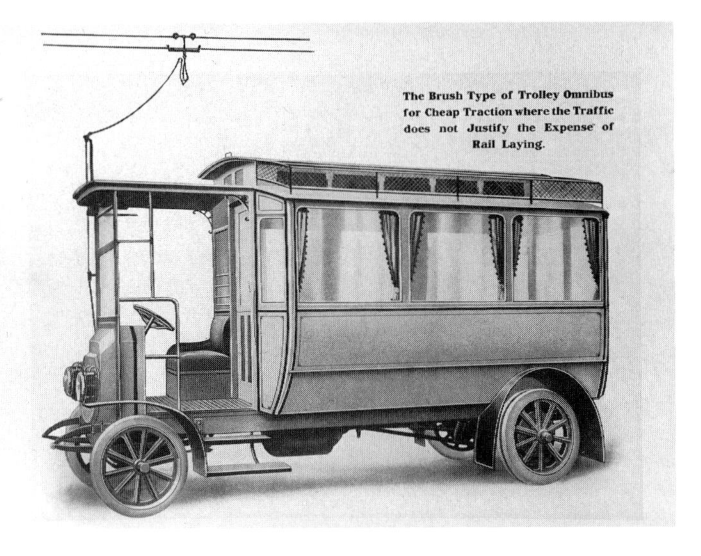

Left:
This is an early Brush advert for trolley-omnibuses. *GLC*

Left:
The first three Brush-built trolley-buses for a British operator were the trio supplied to Stockport Corporation in 1913. Stockport was the only UK system to use the Lloyd-Kohler method of current collection. In 1917 Stockport No 1 was sold to Mexborough & Swinton Tramways to become that operator's No 24. *Brush/GLC*

Left:
In 1914 Brush built six trolleybuses for the Rhondda Tramway Co, again using Daimler chassis frames fitted with Brush traction equipment. These were used only for three months before the service was withdrawn due to the state of the road. In 1920 Clough, Smith & Co purchased these six and resold them to the Teesside Railless Traction Board. *C. Taylor Collection*

Below:
The last three Brush-built trolleybuses were placed in service at Mexborough in August 1915. *Brush/GLC*

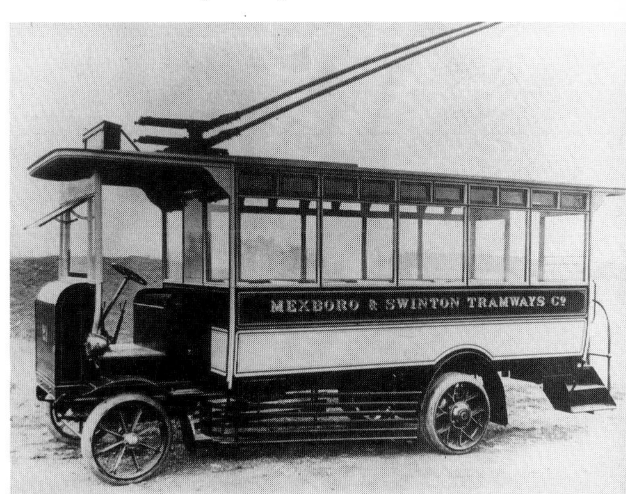

After World War 1 Brush continued to advertise that it could supply complete single-deck trolleybuses but none were sold in Britain. However, in the period from 1922 to 1925, Brush built 24 bodies for Bloemfontein, Georgetown, Keighley and Wigan on Straker-Clough trolleybus chassis.

In an effort to re-enter the trolleybus market the Brush company started in 1930 to build and market vehicles using basic chassis supplied by Thornycroft, which was then having difficulties selling its passenger range of vehicles.

Thornycroft records show that a single-deck petrol chassis with three axles (type FC No 20808) was converted to double-deck specification (type HC) before dispatch to Brush in August 1930. Brush fitted electrical equipment incorporating a Brush light-weight motor and BTH foot-operated control gear embodying electric rheostatic brakes. A Brush 60-seat double-deck body was fitted and in November 1930 it was tested on the nearest trolleybus system at Nottingham. In December 1930 the chassis was renumbered 22422 (type HD) before the vehicle was registered TV3460 for extended trials in passenger service at Nottingham. After six months the vehicle was returned to Brush. The body was purchased by Nottingham for mounting on a new Karrier E6 chassis which entered service in May 1933 as fleet No 1.

Brush sales literature listed four models:

- BD a 27ft 0in long, two-axle, 32/34-seat single-deck
- ID a 26ft 0in long, two-axle, 48/52-seat double-deck
- HD three-axle, 60/64-seat double-deck
- FD a 30ft 0in long, three-axle, single-deck, (data unknown).

Thornycroft records list four chassis numbers, Nos 22420-22423, allocated to trolleybuses in late 1930. Two of these, Nos 22421/22, were model HD, three-axle double-deckers for Derby and the Nottingham demonstrators respectively. The other two were two-axle single and double-deck chassis, presumably the prototypes for models BD and ID. Unfortunately this attempt to produce trolleybuses was not commercially successful and the only other Brush-Thornycroft trolleybus produced was a four-wheel single-decker which was hired for 12 months' experimental service at Bournemouth in 1933, its chassis number being BD 22960. It was registered CG4313 until re-registration as LJ7704 by Bournemouth before entering service.

Incidentally a Thornycroft Cygnet demonstration omnibus was bodied by Brush in late 1932, being fitted with a 32-seat British Electrical Federation standard design body. Yet again this combination failed to attract orders.

Left:
The prototype Brush-Thornycroft three-axle trolleybus built in 1930 was placed in service and tested at Nottingham for six months in 1931. *BTH/GLC*

Below:
Derby Corporation purchased this Brush-Thornycroft trolleybus in 1933. *Ian Allan Library*

Bottom:
In 1933 Bournemouth Corporation hired this Brush-Thornycroft single-deck trolleybus for service on the corporation's experimental route. *Brush/GLC*

7 BUT

British United Traction Ltd

British United Traction Ltd was formed in late 1946 to take over the trolleybus activities of the Associated Equipment Co Ltd and Leyland Motors Ltd. The new company would use the unrivalled experience of both AEC and Leyland to design, manufacture and service all types of trolleybus.

Initially production was based at the former Leyland (Ham) Works in Kingston-upon-Thames.

The double-deck range of vehicles followed AEC practice with the single-deck vehicles being based on a Leyland design. When the electric supply industry was nationalised the cost of power became a burden some operators could not bear. With diminished demand the two 500ft long assembly lines at Kingston had surplus capacity and in 1948, Leyland sold the factory, double-deck vehicles for the home market being built at Southall and single-deck vehicles then being built at Leyland. After ACV (Associated Commercial Vehicles) had absorbed Crossley, AEC-derived BUTs were built at the Crossley factory in Stockport.

In the early 1960s the last BUT orders for export single-deck vehicles were built by Leyland's special-purpose vehicle manufacturing subsidiary, Scammell Lorries Ltd, Watford, for export to Oporto and then for Wellington, New Zealand, in 1964.

Earlier, some BUT chassis had, in the period 1947-1956, been supplied for assembly to Talleres Carde Y Escoriaza, Zaragoza, Spain for bodying. These were then sold as the BUT-Escoriaza trolleybus. The range of models offered allowed a choice of supplier for electrical equipment from five well-known manufacturers: Crompton-Parkinson, English Electric, Metro-Vick, GEC and BTH.

The classification of the earliest BUTs included 961T, 964T and 965T. During 1948 these codes were updated to 9611T, 9641T and 9651T in line with updated type codings for AEC motorbuses. Orders not already completed were given new type codings which meant that some batches of chassis had a mixture of old and new type numbers.

The range of models listed by BUT included:

- 9611T* 26ft 0in long, two-axle, double-deck, built 1947-53
- 9612T 27ft 0in long, two-axle, double-deck, built 1955-56
- 9613T 30ft 0in long, two-axle, double-deck, built 1957-58
- 9641T* 30ft 0in long, three-axle, double-deck, built 1946-56
- 9642T 30ft 0in long, three-axle, double-deck, built 1957-58
- 9651T* 30ft 0in long, three-axle, double-deck, built 1947-50 (LH drive)
- 9652T 30ft 0in long, three-axle, double-deck, built (listed) (LH drive)
- 9711T* 35ft 0in long, two-axle, single-deck, built 1947-53
- 9721T* 35ft 0in long, two-axle, single-deck, built 1947-53 (LH drive)
- RETB1 35ft 0in long, two-axle, single-deck, built 1948-64
- LETB1 35ft 0in long, two-axle, single-deck, built 1950-63 (LH drive)

* models built at Kingston.

The total production of BUT chassis is believed to have been 1,482, comprising 1,092 from AEC and 390 from Leyland factories.

Right:
In late 1947 the first trolleybus to be built by the new company British United Traction Ltd was tested on the Hampton Court route of London Transport. It was the first of the 60 Type 964T trolleybus chassis destined for Johannesburg in South Africa, an operator which had not received 30 AEC 664T trolleybuses earlier due to the war. Of the 30 ordered, 18 completed examples were diverted to London Transport. This vehicle also carried the prototype 8ft-wide body built by Metro-Cammell for the 44 to be assembled in Port Elizabeth by Bus Bodies (SA) Ltd. The remaining 15 bodies were built by British Mining Supplies Co Ltd in Johannesburg to Park Royal designs. BMS was later taken over by J. Brockhouse (SA) Ltd, an associate company of Park Royal. *BUT/GLC*

Left:
The first of Cardiff's 45 BUTs entered service in 1948. They were fitted with East Lancs-built 67-seat dual-door bodies on 9641T chassis. *GEC/GLC*

Right:
London Transport placed the first of its 77 8ft-wide BUT 9641T trolleybuses in service during February 1948. No 1778, one of the first, is shown alongside No 175. The latter was sold in 1955, with four others, to Georgetown, Penang. No 175 was a 1935 AEC 664T. Both carried MCCW bodies. *BUT/GLC*

Left:
In March 1948 the first BUT two-axle trolleybuses of Type 9611T entered service with Brighton, Hove & District. They were fitted with attractive 7ft 6in-wide Weymann bodies and eight similar examples joined the fleet of Brighton Corporation in May 1948. *CP/GLC*

Right:
São Paulo in Brazil was the purchaser of four Weymann-bodied BUT 9721T trolleybuses. They were delivered in 1948, with the chassis being built at Kingston. The bodies were 35ft 6in long and 8ft 6in wide. *BUT/GLC*

Above:
Fifteen BUT 9711T chassis were supplied to Auckland, New Zealand, in 1949. They were fitted with 43-seat dual-doorway bodies by Weymann. A further 40 were supplied in 1951-54 with bodies assembled in New Zealand. *Weymann/GLC*

Right:
Bradford's first BUT 9611T was bodied by C. H. Roe with an 8ft-wide body. It is pictured outside the English Electric Works at Thornbury and entered service in May 1949. *EE/GLC*

Above:
Notts & Derby No 345, another 1949 BUT 9611T, is seen working the trunk route between Ripley and Nottingham among typical traffic of the period. *EE/GLC*

Left:
Belfast's first 24 BUT 9641T trolleybuses were 7ft 6in wide and were supplied complete with lower-deck skeleton framing built by Metal Sections Ltd, Oldbury, for Belfast bodybuilders Harkness to complete. *GEC/GLC*

Right:
Newcastle took delivery in 1948-49 of its first 20 Metro-Cammell-bodied BUT 9641T trolleybuses. These had identical bodies to London's first 'Q1s', even down to the same destination apertures. *EE/GLC*

Right:
The first trolleybuses supplied to Glasgow were 34 70-seat Metro-Cammell-bodied BUT 9641T trolleybuses. Built to the London style — including the LT-type trolleybus motifs. *EE/GLC*

Right:
Newcastle also took delivery of 25 Northern Counties-bodied BUT 9611T trolleybuses. *GEC/GLC*

Left:
To meet the requirements of its direct route to the docks, Cardiff had five of its BUT 9641T trolleybus chassis fitted with single-deck bodies built by East Lancs in 1949. One further example, No 243, followed in 1955. *GEC/GLC*

Left:
Reading No 155 was one of 20 Park Royal-bodied BUT 9611T trolleybuses supplied with platform doors when new in 1949. This view shows one following a speeding cyclist. *EE/GLC*

Below left:
Bradford bought its last six new trolleybuses in January 1951. These were a batch of BUT 9611T trolleybuses fitted with Weymann 8ft-wide bodies. *EE/GLC*

Above:
After 1951 Bradford chose to purchase second-hand trolleybuses, many of which were BUT 9611Ts. These included the 1949-built examples, rebodied by East Lancs, that were third-hand, having originally been bought by Darlington before being sold to Doncaster. This shows one of the type when new to Darlington. *EE/GLC*

Left:
A total of 27 BUT 9651T chassis were supplied to Barcelona without any electrical equipment or motors. The motors and electrical equipment were supplied and fitted by Maquitrans; bodywork was also supplied by a local builder. *GLC*

Above:
Twelve BUT 9641T trolleybuses were assembled by Talleres Carde Y Escoriaza in Zaragoza for San Sebastian a Tolosa SA. Some were fitted with single-deck bodies. According to contemporary adverts three were originally fitted with lorry cabs and dropside bodies for use as goods vehicles. At least one of these lorries was later rebodied as a single-deck trolleybus. *BUT/GLC*

Right:
The last 24 BUT trolleybuses purchased by Belfast were the 8ft-wide 9641T examples. These again carried Harkness bodies built on Metal Section skeleton frames. These entered service in 1953. *Author*

Left:
Glasgow, after buying one single-deck BUT RET1 trolleybus with a Weymann 26-seat standee body, purchased 10 more. These were all 30ft long and were fitted with East Lancs 30ft-long bodies with rear entrance and centre exit. *EE/GLC*

Above:
The only purchasers of the 27ft-long BUT 9612T trolleybus was Manchester, which acquired 62, and Ashton, which acquired eight. The Manchester examples were bodied by Burlingham in 1956-57, whilst those for Ashton were bodied by S. H. Bond in 1956. *MV/GLC*

Right:
Glasgow was the one purchaser of the 30ft-long BUT 9613T trolleybus. The corporation bought 90, which were fitted with Crossley 70- or 71-seat bodies. The batch entered service between July 1957 and January 1959. *Ian Allan Library*

Below:
The General Manager at Glasgow obtained special dispensation to operate 35ft-long single-deck trolleybuses in 1958. The BUT RETB1 chassis was chosen. The vehicles supplied were fitted with a 50-seat front-entrance body built by Burlingham. *Ian Allan Library*

Above:
The first Cedes-Stoll trackless trolley car with Austrian-built chassis and body was supplied on three months' free trial to Keighley where, after official inspection on 24 April 1913, it entered service in May the same year.
GLC

8 Cedes Electric Traction Ltd

The Cedes-Stoll trackless trolley system was based on the Austrian Mercedes-Stoll system developed in 1902 and used from July 1907 at Gmund, Austria. It was marketed from 1910 in this country by Trackless Trolley Ltd, 15-16 Cockspur Street, London SW, who later moved to 112 Great Portland Street, London SW, which also became the home for Cedes-Stoll Electric Traction Ltd.

The Cedes-Stoll (Lohner-Stoll) system of current collection comprised a four-wheel trolley weighing 25lb (12kg) running on top of the two overhead copper cables and which was towed by a flexible cable connected to the trolleybus. Some routes at Keighley and Aberdare were equipped with only one pair of wires which meant that when vehicles met, the two overhead trolleys and flexible cables had to be exchanged.

To coincide with the September 1912 meeting of the Municipal Tramways Association in London a demonstration was made for West Ham Corporation Tramways over a 400yd section of Greengate Street, the vehicle being supplied from Austria with Clough, Smith & Co Ltd erecting the overhead. Clough, Smith & Co Ltd had been active in electrical engineering since it was formed in June 1910, the two partners, Mr Norman Clough and Mr Sidney G. Smith, being involved in erecting the overhead for the 1909 Hendon trials for the Railless Electric Traction Co Ltd.

The trolleybuses incorporated a patented electric motor built into each of the two rear wheels. This had been designed by Mr Ferdinand Porsch, originally for a petrol-electric car and then adapted for electric battery vehicles and trolleybuses both of which were built in the Stamford Hill Works of Cedes Electric Traction Ltd. In 1913 the company was claiming 'that the patented motor, electrical equipment, overhead trolley and chassis are all constructed at their London works', although early examples of the hub motor were built by Johnson and Phillips at their works in Charlton, London.

Following the West Ham trials, Cedes obtained orders from Keighley Corporation and Aberdare UDC, initially supplying the West Ham demonstrator to Keighley through Trackless Trolley Ltd on a free of charge three months' trial which led to further orders. In the meantime contractors Clough, Smith & Co Ltd designed special fittings and erected overhead wiring, crossings and points at the Cedes Stamford Hill Works. It also obtained the contracts for erecting the overhead at Keighley for the trial route, Ingrow to Cross Roads (one mile 1,400yd), at Aberdare (three routes covering three miles 1,000yd), at Keighley further routes (totalling six miles 1,679yd) and finally the 1,000yd experimental line for Hove Corporation from Hove railway station to Church Road. This line was worked by the only Cedes open-top double-deck trolleybus for two months commencing in September 1914.

Cedes supplied a total of 28 trolleybuses — 10 to Keighley including the West Ham and Hove demonstrators, eight to Aberdare and 10 to Germiston in South Africa where, in August 1914, six cars were available for service with the other four delayed due to the South African railways being unable to guarantee delivery due to the war. All the British vehicles except the original West Ham demonstrator were fitted with Christopher Dodson Ltd bodies.

With the outbreak of war with Germany in August 1914, despite claims by Mr K. Bowen, the managing director, that Cedes was a British product, the Cedes Electric Traction Co Ltd was forced into liquidation in 1916. Keighley purchased the overhead from the demonstration line at Hove along with the double-deck trolleybus and a Cedes petrol-electric lorry for the Corporation's refuse department. Clough, Smith erected the last route extension of one mile 1,497yd from Cross Roads to Oxenhope. The war caused great difficulties for all Cedes users and many electrical engineers had to use ingenuity in repairing the Cedes hub motors. In 1921 Keighley had one of its Cedes trolleybuses converted into a tractor-drive by Trackless Cars Ltd from Leeds still using the original Cedes motors.

In Aberdare the last of the three 1921 survivors seems to have expired in mid-1925.

At Keighley the remaining five Cedes trolleybuses had their bodies transferred to new Straker-Clough chassis with one of them retaining the Cedes-Stoll flexible cable and four-wheel trolley for use on the Ingrow-Cross Roads service until May 1926 when this was replaced by a motorbus. So the last section of a Cedes-Stoll trolleybus system in Britain withered away. The system had been novel with hub motors and had complicated overhead trolley current collection which was not suitable for busy routes.

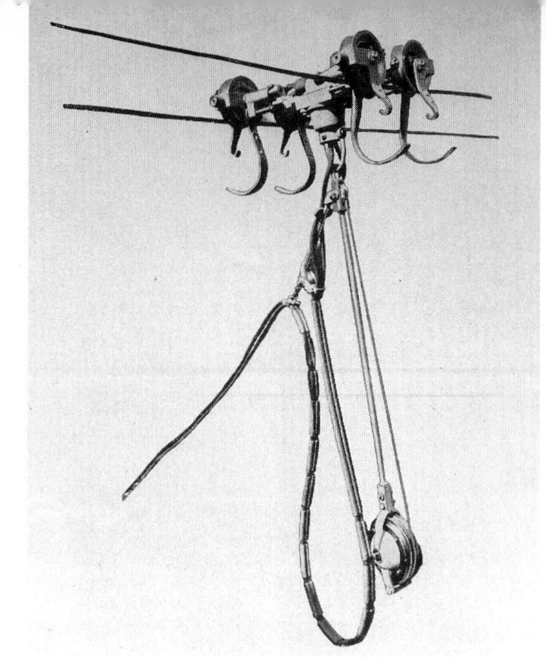

Above:
This shows the Cedes-Stoll method of current collection from the overhead power supply. *GLC*

Below:
A Keighley conductor with red flag warns traffic whilst the drivers exchange current collection trolley and flexible cables. *GLC*

Above:
A view that shows a Cedes-Stoll trolleybus being turned at Keighley. The arrangement allowed the vehicle to manoeuvre, provided that it was within reach of the overhead. *GLC*

Right:
The Aberdare Cedes-Stoll cars, which served the two routes which radiated from the Aberaman tram terminus, wait for passengers from the tram. *GLC*

Left:
A view of the demonstration open-top Cedes-Stoll double-deck trolleybus which operated in Hove for Hove Corporation in late 1914. *GLC*

9 Clough, Smith
Straker-Clough
Karrier-Clough

Clough, Smith and Co Ltd, engineers and contractors, was founded in 1910 when Norman Clough and Sidney G. Smith, both experienced electrical engineers with knowledge of tramway electrification at home and abroad, joined forces to promote the design and installation of suitable overhead power supplies for tramway electrification and for the newly developing trolleybus market. They designed and installed the overhead and traction supplies for all the Cedes-Stoll systems in Britain as well as for some of the other systems for RET Construction Co Ltd. Consequently they suffered somewhat during World War 1 and after a low in 1917-18 when the turnover was £55 1s 1d the company bounced back after completing work on the trolleybus system at Teesside which had been suspended during the war.

This work prompted the company to purchase from the National Electric Construction Co for £7,800 the six Brush trolleybuses which had been stored since March 1915 after only three months' service. Clough, Smith quickly resold these to the Teesside Railless Traction Board for £9,900 and this encouraged the company to exploit this market further. Mr Parker, the General Manager at Teesside, was so pleased with the second-hand Brush-built trolleybuses that he designed 'a trolley omnibus system with an entirely new design of vehicle which embodies all the main features of the tramcar and petrol omnibus with the object of obtaining the very best results, with simplicity and low running cost'. Clough, Smith arranged for its manufacture and marketed it as the Straker-Clough trolley omnibus. They purchased the basic chassis from Straker-Squire Ltd, Edmonton, London, the electrical equipment and motor from BTH at Rugby and arranged in most cases for the body to be built, selling the complete vehicle to the user often as part of a package which included the design, supply and erection of the overhead equipment.

Between October 1921 when the first Straker-Clough entered service at Teesside and September 1926, Clough, Smith sold 63 trolley omnibuses all with solid-tyred wheels.

In November 1926, the first of a new LL model (low loading) fitted with pneumatic tyres was built. It entered service at Rotherham in February 1927, a total of 30 LL models being built before August 1927.

After Straker-Squire Ltd, the supplier of the basic chassis, was voluntarily liquidated on 12 May 1925 and the new company of the same name had to call in the official receiver on 16 July 1926, Clough, Smith had a supply problem. From available records it is known that from the summer of 1925 until the end of May 1927, Clough, Smith & Co Ltd rented buildings from C. H. Roe Ltd at Crossgates, Leeds, paying substantial amounts for rent. What is not clear is what the buildings, which comprised one body shop and the paint shop, were used for. The period involved is concurrent with the Straker-Squire difficulties and one is left to speculate whether the Straker-Clough chassis had the electrical equipment fitted there.

What *is* known is that in the period from July 1921 to June 1928 Clough, Smith & Co Ltd had a turnover of £288,536, 59% of which was from the sale of complete trolleybuses and chassis and a further 17% was from sales of trolleybus overhead, meaning that a total of 76% of the company's turnover was generated by trolleybus-related activities. Clough, Smith therefore had to find another chassis supplier whose product could be adapted for use as a trolley omnibus. They chose to collaborate with Karrier Motors Ltd, Huddersfield, to design the Karrier-Clough Trolley-Omnibus, purchasing electrical equipment from their previous suppliers which meant that all Karrier-Clough trolleybuses had BTH electrical equipment with the exception of the double-deck demonstrator which, when built, had a Bull-made eddy current brake. This new vehicle designated LL was marketed by Clough, Smith and the first customer was Doncaster Corporation which in late 1927 ordered six LL, three-axle, double-deck trolley-omnibuses to which Karrier allocated model type E6.

At the end of 1932, having by then sold 44 Karrier-Clough trolley-omnibuses, including three single-

Left:
The first Straker-Clough trolleybus built for Clough, Smith was sold to Teesside in 1921. It was fitted with a C. H. Roe 36-seat body. *Clough, Smith/GLC*

deck, two-axle vehicles for York, the agreement between Karrier Motors Ltd and Clough, Smith & Co Ltd ended. The last one was supplied as an experimental vehicle to Derby Corporation. Karrier Motors Ltd was then able to market trolleybuses as its own.

Clough, Smith & Co Ltd continued to win contracts for the installation of trolleybus overhead and was still involved as contractor when asked to tender for the removal of the redundant overhead at Reading in 1968-69.

The company has gradually diversified its activities into cable laying, electric flare paths at aerodromes and electrical installations of all kinds including railway resignalling and electrification schemes, overhead and underground power transmission lines and the installation and laying of Mercury fibre-optic cables alongside British Rail tracks. The company is still a leading contractor both at home and for the last 30 years abroad, all a far cry from its 137 pioneering trolley-omnibuses which raised standards and gave the reliability and respectability to enable railless traction to become a serious competitor to the tramway.

Right:
In 1924 Clough, Smith supplied the first trolley-omnibus for Georgetown, Penang. It was fitted with a Brush body that this time incorporated front and rear entrances. This followed an order for Bloemfontein in 1922 which were supplied with rear-entrance Brush bodies. *Clough, Smith and Brush/GLC*

Below:
Also in 1924 Keighley purchased five Straker-Clough chassis from Clough, Smith and fitted existing bodies from the earlier Cedes-Stoll trolleybuses. These bodies had been rebuilt in the early 1920s by C. H. Roe with front entrances. Note the Estler-type trolleybases which permitted unusual trolley alignments. *GLC*

List of Straker-Clough Trolley Omnibuses Sold by Clough, Smith

Date	Qty	Chassis No	BTH Electrical Equipment	Body builder	Customer
10/21	1	1	? – 40hp	Roe B36F	Teesside No 17
5/22*	1	2	GE247H – 40hp	Roe B26F	Rotherham No T2
1/24*	2	3-4	265L – 40hp	Roe B26F	Rotherham Nos T3/T4
8/22	4	5-8	? – 40hp	Roe B36F	Teesside Nos 18-21
8/22	5	9-13	GE247A – ?	Brush	Bloemfontein Nos 11-15 (?)
1/24	1	14		Brush B30D	Georgetown No 1
2/24*	1	15	265L – 1 x 40hp	Existing Dodson used B27F	Keighley No 54
8-9/24*	4	16-19	265L – 1 x 40hp	Existing Dodson used B27F(?)	Keighley Nos 1-4
11/24	6	20-25	265L – 2 x 40hp	Brush H50R	Keighley Nos 5-10
11-12/24	4	26-29	265L – x 40hp	Brush B32F	Keighley Nos 11-14
3/25*	2	30-31	265L	Roe B26F	Rotherham Nos T7/T8
5/25	4	32-35	265L – 1 x 42hp	Brush B37C	Wigan Nos 1-4
10-11/25	4	36-39	265L – 2 x 40hp	Brush H50R	Keighley Nos 15-18
12/25-/26	20	40-59	508A – 1 x 60hp	Roe B31C	Darlington Nos 1-20
9/26	4	60-63	508A – 1 x 60hp	Roe B31C	Darlington Nos 21-24

Following examples are low loading (LL) models which were all fitted with pneumatic tyres from new.

Date	Qty	Chassis No	BTH Electrical Equipment	Body builder	Customer
12/26*	1	64	508B (?) – 1 x 60hp	Roe B32C	Rotherham No 50
12/26-1/27	12	65-76	508A – 1 x 60hp	Vickers B32C	West Hartlepool Nos 8-19
4/27	14	77-90	508A – 1 x 60hp	Reeve & Kenning B32C	Chesterfield Nos 1-12/14/15
10/27*	3	91-93	508B (?) – 1 x 60hp	Roe B32C	Rotherham Nos 47-49

Notes:
* For orders so marked only chassis with electrical equipment supplied.
Total production in six years was 93 chassis; the total value of above was £145,255 6s 10d.

List of Karrier-Clough Trolley Omnibuses Sold by Clough, Smith

Date	Qty	Chassis No	BTH Electrical Equipment	Body builder	Customer
7-9/28	6	54001-6	508D – 66hp	Roe H32/28R	Doncaster Nos 5-10[1]
6-8/29	6	54007-12	508D1 – 66hp	Roe H32/28R	Doncaster Nos 11-16
11/29-3/20	6	54013-18	508D1 – 66hp	Roe H32/28R	Doncaster Nos 17-22[2]
7/30	1	54019	508 – 60hp	Roe H32/28R	Bloemfontein No 5
9/30	1	54020	508D1 – 60hp	Roe H32/28R	Doncaster No 23[2]
3/31	2	54021-22	110B – 77hp	Roe H32/28R	Doncaster Nos H32/28R[3]
10/30	1	54023	508 – 75hp	Park Royal H32/28R	Demonstrator[4, 6]
6-7/31	5	54024-28	110B – 77hp	Roe H32/28R	Doncaster Nos 26-30[3]
9/31	3	55001-3	110E – 65hp	Roe B32R	York Nos 31-33[5, 6]
11/31-1/32	12	54032-43	110D – 80hp	Park Royal H30/30R	Nottingham Nos 25-36
12/32	1	54044	110 – 70hp	Dodson H29/27R	Derby No 99

Notes:
Total sales in five years — 44.
All were Karrier E6 chassis with the exception of Nos 55001-3.
1. Ordered as LL type.
2. Seven ordered. One chassis delayed due to No 54019 going to Bloemfontein.
3. Seven ordered.
4. Demonstrated at Fulwell depot of London United 10/30 then loaned to Nottingham as No 27 until purchased 1/32 as No 50.
5. Chassis Nos 54029-31 voided and new series started as No 55001 for these three E4S model trolleybuses built by Karrier.
6. Supplied complete with bodies by Clough, Smith.

Right:
Keighley also purchased 10 Brush-bodied 50-seat double-deck Straker-Clough' trolley omnibuses. *BTH/GLC*

Below:
Darlington's first Straker-Clough trolley-omnibus is seen outside the works of the bodybuilder, C. H. Roe. *Roe/GLC*

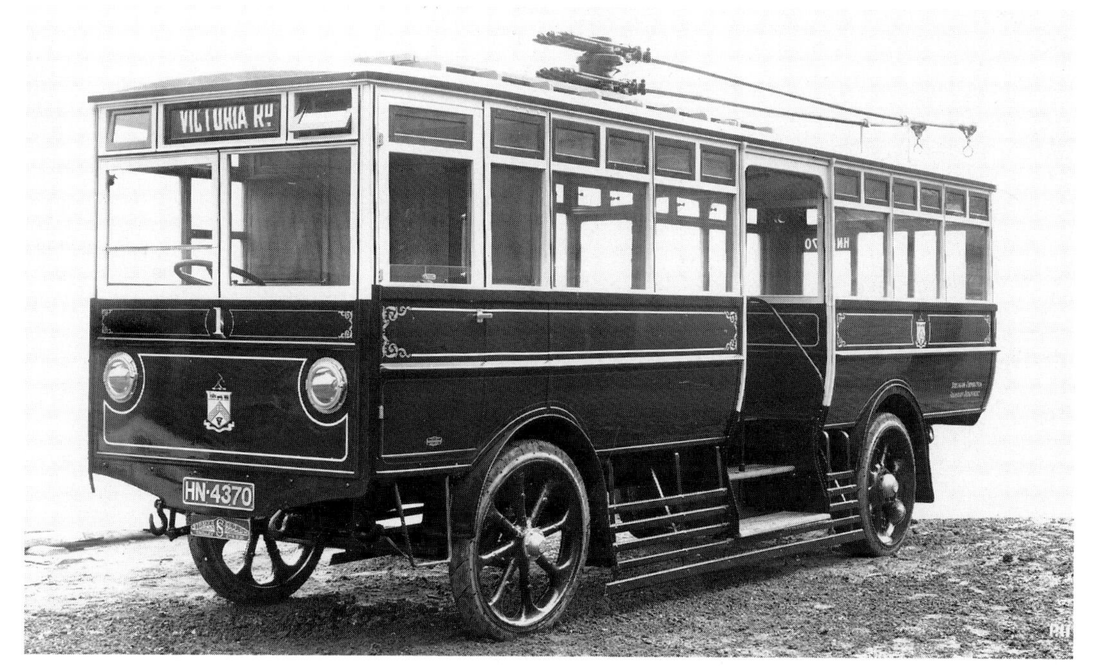

Right:
Rotherham's 1925 Straker-Clough trolley-omnibuses were supplied with front-entrance bodies built by C. H. Roe. These were converted to centre-entrance layout a few years later. *Roe/GLC*

Above:
When West Hartlepool purchased 12 trolley omnibuses fitted with Vickers centre-entrance bodies it represented the first large order for the new Straker-Clough low-loading model (LL) with pneumatic tyres. These 12, delivered in early 1927, were unusual in being operated by West Hartlepool for the 'West Hartlepool and Hartlepool Transport Service' which connected the two towns — the two shared any profit equally. *Clough, Smith/GLC*

Centre left:
The last large order for the Straker-Clough LL model was placed by Chesterfield Corporation, which purchased 14 from Clough, Smith fitted with Reeve & Kenning bodies. The bodies were built at Pilsley, near Chesterfield, and were completed in early 1927.
Reeve & Kenning/GLC

Left:
Rotherham No 49 was the last Straker-Clough trolley-omnibus to be built. It was the 93rd vehicle to be built by the maker and it was appropriate that this, like the first built, was fitted with Roe bodywork.
Roe/GLC

Above:
Wigan's three Brush-bodied trolley-omnibuses supplied in May 1925 were fitted in 1929 with pneumatic tyres on the front wheels only in order to reduce vibration on setted roads. These are the only known trolleybuses to operate with pneumatic tyres on the front wheels and solid tyres on the rear. *GLC*

Above right:
The first LL model double-deck trolleybuses supplied by Clough, Smith were to Doncaster in July 1928. Doncaster, over a period of three years, purchased 26 out of the first 28 Karrier-Clough trolley-omnibuses built. All were fitted with attractive C. H. Roe bodies. *Clough, Smith/GLC*

Below:
In August 1930, after being tested on the Doncaster system, this Karrier-Clough trolley-omnibus was supplied to Bloemfontein in South Africa. It was similar to the Doncaster vehicles and was again bodied by Roe. *Roe/GLC*

Left:
In October 1930 Clough, Smith provided a Karrier-Clough demonstration trolley-omnibus fitted with a Park Royal body. This was hired by London United and tested in its depot at Fulwell before going to Nottingham for evaluation against three demonstrators from Guy, AEC-EE and Brush-Thornycroft. *Park Royal/GLC*

Below:
In October 1931 Clough, Smith supplied three single-deck Karrier-Clough trolley-omnibuses with Roe bodies for York's second attempt at operating trolleybuses. *Roe/GLC*

Left:
In late 1931, as a result of the demonstration at Nottingham, Clough, Smith supplied Nottingham with 12 Karrier-Clough trolley-omnibuses fitted with Park Royal bodies. *Roe/GLC*

Right:
When Derby Corporation started operating trolleybuses in January 1931, Clough, Smith had been the contractor installing the overhead and related equipment. Guy, however, supplied the initial fleet. In 1932 Derby purchased three test vehicles — from Ransomes, Sunbeam and Clough, Smith — none of which changed Derby's purchasing policy. This one, Derby No 99, was Dodson-bodied and was the last Karrier-Clough trolley-omnibus built. *Karrier/GLC*

10 Crossley

The origins of Crossley Motors Ltd go back to 1867 when Crossley Brothers Ltd started to manufacture gas engines and gas plant. In 1910 Crossley Motors Ltd was formed to manufacture luxury cars and be involved in motor racing which were activities in conflict with Crossley Brothers business. In 1928 it started the manufacture of full-sized motorbuses, quickly persuading Manchester City Council that by supporting local manufacturers it gave employment to Manchester citizens as well as generating rate revenue. From late 1930 to 1937 only 22 out of the 350 motorbuses purchased by Manchester in that period were not Crossley-built. So in April 1935, when the city council proposed introducing trolley-buses in Manchester, despite opposition by the manager, it was not surprising that Crossley were quick to respond and by late October 1935 it announced that the company was entering the trolleybus market.

Models produced between then and 1951 comprised TDD6 (trolleybus, double-deck, six-wheel), a three-axle design with an 18ft 7in wheel-base and 95hp MV motor, and TDD4 (trolleybus, double-deck, four-wheel). Seventeen TDD6s were built including the prototype which was modified to accept the larger 95hp motor (instead of the 80hp motor originally fitted). Twelve of these went to Manchester, three to Ashton and two to Belfast. The TDD4 design were two-axle vehicles with a 16ft wheelbase. In all 97 TDD4s were built. Ashton took the prototype and eight others, 68 went to Manchester and 20 were supplied in 1938 to Kingston-upon-Hull. The last TDD4 was delivered to Manchester during 1943. Of these 114 prewar Crossley trolleybuses, Crossley finished the bodies on all except one TDD6 for Belfast and 20 TDD4s for Kingston-upon-Hull. As a result, 93 had bodies completed by Crossley on MCCW frames.

After the war the first order for trolleybuses was received in June 1945, when 10 TSD42/1 single-deck 'Transit' model, two-axle trolleybus chassis suitable for 40 seats plus 32 standee bodies, 33ft 7in long, were ordered by the municipality of Wellington in New Zealand. A further four for delivery to New Zealand were ordered by the New Plymouth municipality.

The first British customer after the war was Manchester which in 1946 ordered 54 trolleybuses complete with bodies comprising 38 TDD42/1s and 16 TDD64/1s. This was followed by Ashton who ordered five Crossley-bodied TDD42/2s. The final trolleybus chassis order received was for two TDD42/3s for Cleethorpes UDC which were the only two postwar vehicles not to have Crossley-built all-metal bodies. The model designations postwar expanded to include the number of driven wheels as well as minor variations (eg /1). A typical specification was TDD42/2 (trolleybus, double-deck, four wheels, two driven, variation 2.

In early 1947 production was moved from Gorton to the former aircraft shadow factory No 6 at Errwood Park, Stockport, a few hundred yards outside the Manchester boundary. Production problems and lack of orders for motorbuses from Manchester caused acute financial difficulties, which were eventually solved when AEC Ltd purchased the share capital of Crossley Motors Ltd in August 1948. At the same time the new parent company changed its name to ACV Ltd (Associated Commercial Vehicles Ltd). Profit turned to loss and by June 1951 the new parent

Left:
The prototype Crossley three-axle trolleybus chassis was built for display at the 1935 Commercial Motor Show, after which it was fitted with a body built by Crossley using MCCW framing. After testing over the short Ashton-under-Lyne Corporation route in June 1936 it went to Newcastle for two weeks in July for testing on behalf of the manufacturers over a route similar to the proposed Stalybridge-Ashton-Manchester service, over which it was planned to introduce trolleybuses. These tests, in intensive traffic conditions which were not possible over the existing Ashton route, established that the vehicle was underpowered for the proposed schedules in Manchester; it was planned to reduce the time from the journey over the 6.5 mile route between Ashton and Manchester by 11min. *Crossley/GLC*

company decided to cease marketing the Crossley chassis.

Efforts were then made to expand body production and the new management obtained orders for both motor and trolleybus bodies, the latter being from Bradford City Transport for 13 new bodies on refurbished AEC and Karrier two-axle prewar trolleybus chassis. The works then assembled trolleybus chassis for British United Traction Ltd, a joint AEC and Leyland company. These included the 70 9612Ts built for Manchester and Ashton, the 90 9613Ts supplied to Glasgow, and 9641Ts for Cardiff and Huddersfield.

Some of the 90 chassis for Glasgow had bodies subcontracted to Crossley by Park Royal Vehicles Ltd, another member of the ACV group, hence the PRV body plate. The last one was delivered to Glasgow on 4 December 1958.

In November 1957 Crossley Motors Ltd was made a dormant company and what remained of the Crossley Motors business became the Crossley Division of AEC Ltd; most of the remaining staff were made redundant in early 1958. So another manufacturer involved with trolleybuses bit the dust having produced a total of 189 chassis of its own design and built 250 trolleybus bodies as well as assembling at least 198 BUT chassis.

Below left:
In 1936 Crossley built its prototype two-axle trolleybus, which was exhibited at the Scottish Motor Show in November that year. This led to orders from Manchester Corporation, which chose the two-axle model for the basic services, with the three-axle types being used for short workings and peak periods. *Crossley/GLC*

Top right:
No 1055 is typical of the production three-axle chassis produced by Crossley and supplied to Manchester Corporation. *GLC*

Centre right:
Hull was the only non-Manchester area operator prewar to purchase Crossley two-axle trolleybuses. The corporation purchased 20 fitted with bodies supplied by Cravens in 1938. *Cravens/GLC*

Below:
Belfast was the only operator outside the Manchester area to purchase Crossley three-axle trolleybuses. In 1938 the corporation purchased trial vehicles from seven suppliers, including Crossley. One of the two Crossley examples, No 3 had a Crossley-built body; it is shown being loaded at Liverpool. *Ian Allan Library*

Left:
Manchester No 1144 was one of the last prewar Crossley trolley-buses to be supplied, being delivered in early 1940. *Ian Allan Library*

Below:
In 1951 Crossley supplied 16 three-axle trolleybuses, of type TDD64/1, to Manchester for use on peak duties and short workings. Here No 1253 approaches the Manchester boundary from Denton on the trunk road across the Pennines from Sheffield. *Author*

Left:
In 1950 Ashton purchased five two-axle TDD42/2 trolleybuses from Crossley for its share of joint services with Manchester. *Author*

Right:
Cleethorpes Corporation in 1951 purchased two two-axle TDD42/3 trolleybuses fitted with Roe bodies. These were to be the only Crossley trolleybuses to operate for more than one operator. Cleethorpes was taken over in 1957 by Grimsby-Cleethorpes Transport, which sold the batch in 1960 to Walsall Corporation. Walsall was itself absorbed by the West Midlands Passenger Transport Executive in 1969. *Author*

11 Daimler

After the break-up of The Associated Daimler Co Ltd in July 1928, the Daimler Motor Co Ltd of Coventry continued to produce its own petrol-engined bus and coach chassis for expanding markets at home and abroad.

In early 1936 Daimler appointed Mr F. A. Garrett MIAE in a consultative and advisory capacity to design two- and three-axle trolleybus chassis. He had been with Ransomes until 1932 when he moved to Leyland to expand Leyland manufacture to include trolleybuses.

In late 1936 the owners of Daimler, BSA Ltd, formed a new subsidiary company, Transport Vehicles (Daimler) Ltd, to deal with the company's expanding business in transport including trolleybuses.

Daimler built its first trolleybus chassis in late 1936 and thus became the last British manufacturer to enter the trolleybus market. A contemporary article stated 'when a concern such as the Daimler Co Ltd, Coventry, enters a new field of activity, it may be taken for granted that the type of vehicle offered is bound to be an attractive proposition. This is certainly so in the case of the trolleybus, for the mechanical components are soundly designed and beautifully finished. Whilst a guarantee of quality is assured by the mere fact that the standardised equipment is of Metropolitan Vickers make. The new trolleybus chassis is not an adaptation of the concern's petrol or oil-engined chassis but has been designed throughout to meet the special service conditions which are peculiar to this type of vehicle. Realising that municipalities have individual ideas as to the most desirable equipment, the Daimler engineers have so planned the chassis that the requirements of almost any specification can be met without engendering a great deal of attention to the standard components'.

Despite this impressive specification and the availability of free of charge demonstrators, Daimler had

Right:
In 1942, following enemy action, South Shields had to replace the Willowbrook body on the prototype with a new utility body supplied by Roe. *Roe/GLC*

built only 25 trolleybuses when World War 2 broke out and manufacture had to be suspended to carry out war work. These included the two CTM4s, and the CTM6 prototypes, 14 CTM4 models for West Hartlepool, six for Derby and two CTM6 models for Belfast — all established Daimler motorbus users. After the war, Daimler sold a further 92 trolleybuses, all of them three-axle CTM, CTC or CTE6 chassis, with Rotherham taking 44 CTC and CTE6 single-deckers, Glasgow 30 CTM6 double-deckers and, the only export order Daimler received, 18 CTM6 double-deckers for Pretoria, South Africa.

The designation of the models was based on a simple code:

eg CTM4:
C = Commercial; T = Trolleybus;
M = Metropolitan-Vickers electrical equipment;
4 = four wheels.

The postwar specifications included electrical equipment by English Electric (E) and Crompton-Parkinson (C).

Right:
The prototype Daimler CTM6 was supplied to Newcastle in March 1938 free of charge for trials before being purchased by the Corporation. It carried a dual-staircase MCCW body. *John Aldridge Collection*

Left:
The only other two three-axle Daimler CTM6s to be built before 1939 were the pair supplied to Belfast, which entered service in 1938. They were fitted with Harkness bodies. *Daimler/GLC*

Right:
After the war Rotherham placed orders for a total of 44 Daimler CTE6 and CTC6 trolleybuses with East Lancs bodywork for 38 seats. Eight of these were built at Blackburn with the remainder coming from a subsidiary, East Lancs (Bridlington) Ltd. Delivery took place between 1949 and 1951. No 91 was one of the English Electric-equipped examples. *EE/GLC*

Above:
Derby purchased six Brush-bodied Daimler CTM4s in 1938. They represented the operator's first two-axle trolleybuses. It is interesting to note that the batch retained the two steps to the platform which had been necessary on the three-axle Guys. *Brush/GLC*

Above:
When Rotherham changed its policy, 20 of the single-deck Daimler CTE6s were rebodied with new Roe 70-seat double-deck bodies. *Roe/GLC*

Below:
Glasgow was the only other British purchaser of Daimler trolleybuses postwar. It purchased 30 CTM-DDs in 1950. These were fitted with MCCW 70-seat bodies. *Metrovick/GLC*

12 EMB

The Electro Mechanical Brake Co Ltd of West Bromwich, which started in 1923 to supply Birmingham Corporation Tramways with bogies for over 200 tramcars, built in 1924 a unique, low-floor, double-deck trolleybus for Birmingham.

To achieve this, each rear wheel was driven by separate motors mounted outside the chassis frame. The electrical equipment, ordered from English Electric Co Ltd in August 1923, comprised two DK 85A, 42HP motors and a type D hand controller which were identical to the equipment supplied by EE to Railless Ltd for the 12 double-deck trolleybuses supplied in 1921 and the three later ones built in 1925 also by Railless. The motors drove by cardan shafts and universal joints to worm wheels and gears bolted to each rear wheel.

The low-height body was built in Leeds by C. H. Roe (1923) Ltd and had an enclosed rear platform with low step and entrance platform; seating 20 downstairs and 28 upstairs.

It ran in service for less than two years before being withdrawn in 1926 after clocking up approximately 30,000 miles.

Above:
This example of the EMB low-floor trolleybus was built for Birmingham. It was fitted with a low-height Roe 48-seat body with low step entrance. *Roe/GLC*

Right:
The EMB low-floor trolleybus chassis, built in 1923, shows the twin English Electric motors mounted outside the frame. *Ian Allan Library*

13 English Electric

In 1919 five well-known pioneers in the electrical industry were consolidated into a new company — The English Electric Co Ltd. Amongst these were the Dick, Kerr works at Preston, the Phoenix works at Bradford and the Siemens works at Stafford. These companies had been involved with the manufacture and supply of electrical equipment for trolleybuses since 1911 when Siemens motors and equipment were used for the Bradford and Leeds trolleybuses. Dick, Kerr & Co Ltd had also built tramcars, railway rolling stock and bodies for road vehicles through its subsidiary company United Electric Car Co Ltd.

The major user of motors and equipment for trolleybuses was Railless Ltd which ceased manufacture in 1926. EEC, concerned at this potential loss of work, stepped in to supply complete railless vehicles using a commercially available motorbus chassis as the base. EEC ordered for a sum of £495 a basic chassis for experimental purposes from Leyland Motors Ltd on 6 October 1926; at that time a complete chassis cost £875. By 28 January 1927, EEC had designed a suitable body with rear entrance and 31 seats. After this had been built at Preston the vehicle was tested at Ashton-under-Lyne in the summer of 1927, where it was reported to have regularly carried up to 65 passengers! Records show minor changes were made to the electrical specification and then, after Bradford had invited offers for the supply of 10 centre entrance, single-deck trolleybuses, EEC rebuilt the body with a wide centre entrance to speed loading, and at the same time changed the type of controller and fitted rheostatic braking. This altered trolleybus was demonstrated at Maidstone in July 1928.

Following the success of this experimental railless vehicle, EEC built a further 39 single-deck, two-axle trolleybuses at first using Leyland chassis frames and then its own. To meet the demand for larger vehicles EEC delivered, in August 1929, the first three-axle double-deck vehicles ordered by Bradford. These measured 14ft 10in in height. A total of 53 three-axle chassis were supplied; all except six had EEC single- or double-deck bodies. The exceptions were the ones supplied to Christchurch, New Zealand, which had the front axle set back to allow a front entrance. The single-deck bodies for them were designed by EEC but to save shipping charges were built in New Zealand.

In March 1930 after AEC and EEC joined forces to market trolleybuses, customers had the option of purchasing EEC-built vehicles with the motor mounted amidship or the AEC product where the motor was fitted at the front of the chassis, so allowing the overall height of a double deck vehicle to be over 9in lower than the pure EEC example.

EEC continued to call trolleybuses 'railless vehicles' into the 1930s, a long time after Railless Ltd had ceased to manufacture.

The last EEC-built trolleybus was completed in August 1931 for Bradford which, not surprisingly, had purchased 53 out of the total of 93 EEC-built trolleybuses, as the traction equipment was built at the Phoenix works, Bradford.

The joint venture between English Electric and AEC was a successful combination of mechanical and electrical expertise but, despite this, many users preferred alternative body builders to EEC.

Below:
The prototype English Electric trolleybus pictured as built with rear-entrance body ready to go to Ashton for initial trials in the summer of 1927. *EE/GLC*

Right:
After initial trials the prototype was rebuilt with a centre entrance for improved passenger flow for further trials at Ashton in late 1928.
EE/GLC

Left:
The 16 production English Electric trolleybuses purchased by Bradford in 1928-29 had English Electric-built bodies of improved appearance incorporating doors at the top of the stairs to meet MoT requirements. *EE/GLC*

Right:
Bradford was the first customer for the three-axle English Electric-built and bodied double-deck trolleybuses. No 572 was the first of 25 delivered between 1929 and 1932.
EE/GLC

Left:
Nottingham also placed six English Electric double-deck trolleybuses in service in early 1930. This fine shot shows a trolleybus taking evasive action to avoid an emerging car. *Chris Taylor/GLC*

Above:
When Pontypridd introduced trolleybuses in 1930 it purchased seven single-deck three-axle English Electric trolleybuses. Here six of the fleet wait at the depot at Treforest for their next turn of duty. *EE/GLC*

Left:
In July 1930 Southend purchased a pair of English Electric dual-entrance trolleybuses with a single low-step rear platform. *EE/GLC*

Right:
The only export order received by English Electric for its trolleybuses was from Christchurch in New Zealand, which ordered six single-deck chassis with a set back front axle for a forward-entrance body. To save shipping costs English Electric designed a body suitable for construction in New Zealand. A mock-up cab layout was built for testing a weighted chassis at Preston. This view also shows the trailing skate used. *EE/GLC*

Left:
During 1931 Bradford took delivery of its penultimate three-axle double-deck English Electric trolleybus. This view of No 595 shows the final design of bodywork. *EE/GLC*

Right:
The last English Electric-designed and built single-deck trolleybus was constructed for Notts & Derby. The batch of six with 32 seat bodies did not enter service until January 1932. *EE/GLC*

14 Garrett

The introduction of trolleybuses in Ipswich in September 1923 inspired two Suffolk manufacturers to expand their range of products to include trolleybuses in an effort to encourage Ipswich to purchase locally-made products. One of these manufacturers was Richard Garrett & Sons Ltd of Leiston which was a member of the Agricultural & General Engineers Ltd group of companies. This group also included Bull Motors Ltd which manufactured all the motors fitted to Garrett trolleybuses at its works in Ipswich.

Garrett completed an experimental railless trolleybus chassis in February 1925. It was built with a high straight frame and it had pressed steel disc wheels with solid tyres and rear wheel brakes only. The rear axle was fitted with a David Brown worm and wheel. The electrical equipment comprised a Bull 50hp motor and a Garrett foot-operated controller. The 26ft long chassis was sent to C. H. Roe (1923) Ltd at Leeds for a 32-seat centre-entrance body to be fitted. The trolleybus was then tested at Leeds, Keighley and Bradford before arriving in Ipswich on 16 July 1925 for extended trials which lasted until March 1926 when the first of the 15 25ft-long, Strachan & Brown-bodied, 31-seat dual-entrance trolleybuses arrived.

Meanwhile a second prototype was built, this time with a low loading line chassis. This was fitted with a Strachan & Brown, 36-seat, centre-entrance body and was displayed at the Commercial Motor Show at Olympia in November 1925 before being demonstrated on the Mexborough & Swinton system in December. In early 1926 it entered service for extended trials at Leeds before being purchased by Bradford in November 1926.

Both these prototypes were well received and production orders were received for three types of single-deck vehicles all of model type 0. Ipswich purchased 15 solid-tyred, 13ft 6in short wheelbase chassis, allowing a forward entrance but still having rear wheel brakes only. The most popular was the centre-entrance-bodied model on the 15ft 6in wheelbase chassis.

The third variation was the short wheelbase chassis on pneumatic-tyred wheels, with front entrance all fitted with a 50hp Bull motor and BTH contactor type controller. Despite offering a double-deck version of

Left:
A July 1925 scene in Keighley shows the prototype Garrett trolleybus, fitted with Roe bodywork, being demonstrated to council officials. *Garrett/GLC*

Left:
The second Garrett trolleybus, built in late 1925, was displayed at the 1925 Commercial Motor Show in Ipswich livery. *Garrett/GLC*

Right:
In early 1926 this second Garrett trolleybus was used for extended trials in Leeds. It carried the Leeds coat of arms, as seen in this illustration of it returning from New Farnley to Leeds City Square. The vehicle was fitted with a Strachan & Brown body. *Garrett/GLC*

Below:
Ipswich's first large order for trolleybuses, in 1926, included 15 solid-tyred Garretts with a set back front axle for front-entrance bodywork supplied by Strachan & Brown. *Garrett/GLC*

the standard O-type with solid-tyred wheels and a 57-seat body, no orders were received.

For the November 1927 Commercial Motor show at Olympia Garrett displayed a model 'OS' three-axle double-deck trolleybus. This was 26ft 7in long and fitted with a Garrett 55-seat metal-framed body. The chassis was fitted with a 60hp Bull double-wound motor and BTH series-parallel control. Orders for a further nine OS model trolleybuses were received; four of these went to Doncaster Corporation who had them fitted with 60-seat bodies. The first one was completed by C. H. Roe Ltd on 25 March 1928 on chassis No 387. It was tested in late March on trade plates over part of the nearby Mexborough & Swinton system between Conisbrough and Manvers Main before being registered on 3 April as DT821. Roe records listed chassis numbers 388, 389 and 386 as Doncaster Nos 2, 3 and 4 respectively.

The OS exhibition vehicle was purchased by Southend, after having been on hire to that operator. In February 1929 Southend purchased a further five OS models, this time with 60-seat Garrett bodies; these being delivered between May and June 1929.

In May 1929 Garrett produced an impressive 52-page catalogue. It appeared that Garrett was going to continue to be a major builder. Surprisingly therefore that only a repeat order for three type O single-deck trolleybuses for Mexborough & Swinton was received after this brochure was published. However, it is known that trolleybus manufacture was not showing much profit. This was partly due to having to purchase components from outside suppliers, which meant that only assembly work and the building of occasional bodies was done at Leiston and this resulted in high overheads. This, when coupled with the fact that the specifications needed updating since the Karrier-Clough trolleybuses entering service in Doncaster at the same time as the four Garretts had a floor height of 2ft 1in (9in lower than the Garrett examples), all meant that in late 1930 Garrett decided to withdraw from trolleybus manufacture.

Garrett's decision led to Bull Motors Ltd supplying a Bull eddy current brake to the Karrier-Clough demonstrator and a Bull motor to the second Bristol demonstrator, both built in 1930. Garrett went into receivership at the beginning of 1932 having sold its last trolleybus, the former continental demonstrator, to Ipswich on 24 November 1931 after first converting it to right-hand drive. This last trolleybus brought the total built by Garrett to 101 over a period of five years.

Above:
In 1927 West Hartlepool took delivery of 12 Roe-bodied Garrett trolleybuses for its own trolleybus routes. *Garrett/GLC*

Right:
Roe also built bodies for six Garrett trolleybuses exported to Lima Light Power & Tramways Co of Peru. The vehicles were tested on the Leeds routes, and this view of No 3 was taken at Burley-in-Wharfedale on 17 December 1927. *Roe/GLC*

Above:
Garrett built its first double-deck three-axle trolleybus with an all-metal body for display at the 1927 Commercial Motor Show. After the show it was tested at Southend, before being purchased by that operator in February 1929. *Garrett/GLC*

Right:
The final three Garrett trolleybuses, built in 1930, were for Mexborough & Swinton Traction Co and were numbered 61-3. No 61 is shown new with the trolley gear removed prior to dispatch by LNER train to the customer. It was customary to leave the bamboo pole on top of the vehicle with other items being sent loose or in packing cases inside the vehicle. *Garrett/GLC*

Right:
Doncaster purchased four Roe-bodied Garrett rigid three-axle trolleybuses for its first tram to trolleybus conversions. This view of No 1 was taken at Doncaster on 3 May 1928. *Roe/GLC*

Below:
Southend placed five Garrett-bodied rigid three-axle trolleybuses in service during the summer of 1929. The vehicles were fitted with an enclosed staircase body. *Garrett/GLC*

Left:
The Gilford-ECC trolleybus was ready for simulated tests in September 1932 and was tested over the Wolverhampton system.
John Aldridge Collection

15 Gilford-ECC

Probably the most ingenious and revolutionary trolleybus to be produced was the result of the Gilford Motor Co Ltd, of High Wycombe, joining forces with the Electric Construction Co Ltd, of Wolverhampton.

During 1932 the two companies converted the Gilford low-height, chassisless, double-deck bus, which had been the star of the 1931 Commercial Motor show at Olympia, into a trolleybus. This vehicle had been designed to be fitted with a Junkers oil engine and incorporated front-wheel drive and independent air suspension for the front wheels. It was also fitted with four single pneumatic tyres. The chassisless construction allowed a totally flat floor only 1ft 2in above the road surface for the rear platform and lower saloon. The overall height was 12ft 11in with conventional centre gangways in both saloons, which seated 22 downstairs and 28 upstairs. The metal framed body, 26ft long, was built by Wycombe Motor Bodies Ltd, an associate company of Gilford. As this bus was a totally new concept it had failed to attract orders. So, in an attempt to recover its development costs, the rapidly growing market for trolleybuses seemed to provide an answer.

ECC provided a 70bhp traction motor capable of giving the vehicle a maximum speed of 32mph. This motor was fitted behind the front wheels and protruded into the lower saloon, necessitating a single seat either side of it at the front of the lower saloon. The ECC control equipment was housed in the driver's cab and was accessible through the front dash.

During September 1932, having carried out simulated tests, it was arranged that the vehicle would be placed into passenger service on the Wolverhampton Corporation trolleybus system for extended trials. It was then registered as JW2347 and ran in public service for the last six weeks of 1932.

This unique vehicle then seems to have disappeared from the public scene and Gilford's attempts to sell advanced vehicle design to the conservative transport industry contributed to its own failure in 1935 during the depression of the 1930s. The next chassisless trolleybus was produced by the London Passenger Transport Board in 1937. The front-wheel drive concept was eventually accepted in the late 1950s with the Austin/Morris Mini.

16 Gloster

In 1933 the Gloucester Railway Carriage & Wagon Co Ltd designed and produced a trolleybus, type TDD, with a 54-seat all-metal double-deck centre-entrance body. It was shown from 2-11 November at the 1933 Commercial Motor Show at Olympia.

In previous years the company, established in 1860, had produced single-deck horse-drawn tramcars, horse-drawn open-top double-deck buses, electric cabs in 1898 for the London Electric Cab Co, the gantry cars for the Brighton & Rottingdean Seashore Co, bodies for Clarkson steamers as well as a large variety of horse-drawn vehicles. The company had also fitted bodies to three-axle petrol-driven lorries for the War Department in the late 1920s.

Unfortunately, the company was one of the victims of the collapse of the private owner railway rolling stock interests of H. G. Lewis & Co. Henry Lewis himself, the head of this company, had been a director of Gloucester since late 1924. During early 1929, Gloucester purchased a controlling interest in H. G. Lewis & Co. Then, when the British coal trade suffered a sudden depression in 1930, its investment became worthless and the company reserves were reduced by 70%. At the same time, H. G. Lewis was chairman of Northern Counties Motor & Engineering Co Ltd and a director of Hall Lewis & Co Ltd, Park Royal, London. In addition, a Mr H. G. Lewis (junior) held the position of Secretary to NCME as well as being a director of Hall Lewis & Co Ltd. Hall Lewis & Co was taken over on 12 April 1930 by a new company, Park Royal Coachworks Ltd.

In an effort to ensure that the Gloucester company was to survive, the MP for Gloucester, Mr Leslie Boyce, became chairman at the end of 1931. Mr Boyce, who later became a Lord Mayor of London, was a professional financier who took steps to diversify the company's activities. The company normally exported 85% of its works output, but the lack of this export business in 1933, when no orders were received, caused the company to consider the production of complete vehicles for road use. These included building the prototype Gloster-Gardner single-deck coaches and the Gloster TDD (trolleybus, double deck) which was the first trolleybus built with the lightweight Crompton-Parkinson 75hp motor fitted behind the rear axle. This allowed the 54-seat all-metal body to have a low centre gangway and centre entrance, 1ft 2in from the ground. The control gear was supplied by Allan West & Co Ltd and was accessible by removing half of the front panelling.

After the show it was hired to Southend for 12 months, being registered JN3822. Southend purchased it in December 1934 and continued to operate it until the end of 1950, having very little trouble with it in its 17 years of service, during which it covered 402,242 miles. The main problems were associated with differential and worm shaft bearing failures, electrical problems being minimal.

This attempt by Gloucester to enter a new market was not repeated since it was not financially viable and the company did not believe in working at a loss. The fortunes of Gloucester improved dramatically in 1936 when it began to receive rearmament orders and in 1937 it received orders from the London Passenger Transport Board valued at over £1.5 million for tube trains.

The design of the Gloster trolleybus was well thought out and was 15 years ahead of its time with its rear motor anticipating the rear-engined motorbuses of the late 1950s. It was the most successful design of any prototype from a manufacturer which had not been involved in the industry before.

Above:
The one and only Gloster trolleybus chassis was built with a cranked nearside chassis frame for a low central entrance. The Crompton-Parkinson traction motor was mounted behind the rear axle. *John Aldridge Collection*

Below:
The completed Gloster trolleybus is pictured before it went for display at the 1933 Commercial Motor Show. After the show it went on hire to Southend before being purchased by that operator in December 1934. *GLC*

17 Guy

Guy Motors Ltd, Fallings Park, Wolverhampton, was the first manufacturer to build a three-axle double-deck motorbus. It was 26ft long, fitted with pneumatic tyres and had a low frame which allowed a floor height of 2ft 3in in the lower saloon of the Dodson-built body. Some of the credit for its development lay with Owen Silvers, the General Manager of Wolverhampton Corporation, who took delivery of the first vehicle in July 1926. Silvers was faced with providing replacement vehicles for some of the town's trams and was already operating a large fleet of petrol-electric Tilling-Stevens motorbuses as well as 32 single-deck Tilling-Stevens trolleybuses. Being impressed with this new motorbus he saw the potential for a similar-sized trolleybus for tramway replacement. He persuaded Mr W. A. Stevens, who had been involved with the original development of the Tilling-Stevens petrol-electrics, to work with Guy and Rees Roturbo Co Ltd, another Wolverhampton concern. Guy adapted a standard three-axle motorbus chassis for trolleybus work, with the most important feature of the vehicle being the electrical equipment. This was known as the Rees-Stevens electric system in which a single 60hp Rees-Stevens motor with regenerative control manufactured by the Rees Roturbo Co Ltd, was fitted at the front of the chassis. The vehicle was tested at Wolverhampton in December 1926. Owen Silvers, delighted with the vehicle's performance, continued to expand his trolleybus fleet at Wolverhampton by purchasing further vehicles until there were 59 Guy BTX trolleybuses in service by early 1933, when he purchased the first Sunbeam trolleybuses also built in Wolverhampton. Other early users of the BTX model were HastingsTramways Co with 50 single-deck and eight open-top double-deck examples, and Rotherham with five.

A two-axle version of the BTX was introduced in 1930 as model BT. This was built as a 26ft-long double-decker, a 27ft-long single-decker or as a shorter 23ft-long single-decker for export to Delhi.

In 1935 the first of the 30ft-long BTX model appeared, with examples of both double-deck and single-deck being built for Newcastle and Rotherham respectively.

By 1933 Guy held the patents and manufacturing rights for the electrical equipment which was built for them by Electrical Construction Co, Wolverhampton. All trolleybuses built continued to use front-mounted motors which were available in various sizes up to 100hp.

At the outbreak of World War 2, Guy had built 376 trolleybus chassis. Manufacture was suspended until 1947 when the two postwar orders were built. These were for Belfast, which purchased 70 BTX model, 30ft-long trolleybuses with GEC equipment, and Wolverhampton, which ordered 50 BT model, 26ft-long trolleybuses with BTH electrical equipment. At this point Guy had built 496 trolleybus chassis with the first and last ones being delivered to Wolverhampton.

In October 1948, Guy purchased the business and the Moorfields works of the Sunbeam Trolleybus Co Ltd from Brockhouse & Co Ltd. In view of the increased demand at Fallings Park for motorbuses and lorries, the decision was taken to produce all future trolleybuses under the Sunbeam name, discontinuing the manufacture of the two Guy models.

In 1953 Guy Motors closed the Moorfields works

Left:
This vehicle is typical of the 16 Guy trolleybuses built for Wolverhampton in 1927 with Dodson 61-seat bodies. The bodies, which were 26ft long, possessed enclosed staircases, unlike the prototype No 33.
John Aldridge Collection

Above:
The Hastings Tramways Co introduced trolleybuses in April 1928 to replace its tramways. The first eight trolleybuses were Guy BTXs with open-top Dodson bodies. This view is of No 3 when new. *Guy/GLC*

Below:
The major part of the Hastings Tramways Co's trolleybus fleet was represented by 50 Guy BTX single-deck trolleybuses built with Ransomes bodies. No 50 was supplied in 1929. *Guy/GLC*

Left:
When the South Lancashire Transport Co started replacing its trams with trolleybuses, the first vehicles it received were Guy BTXs fitted with 60-seat lowbridge double-deck bodies built by Roe. This fine shot of No 1 was taken outside the Roe works in June 1930. *Roe/GLC*

Right:
Walsall No 10 was a 1931 Guy BTX trolleybus fitted with a Brush body. It was renumbered 154 before entering service. *Ian Allan Library*

Left:
Guy Motors was successful in gaining all the early batch orders placed by Derby Corporation, which chose to acquire BTXs. No 82 was placed in service during January 1932 and was fitted with a 56-seat Brush body. *Guy/GLC*

and transferred trolleybus production to Fallings Park where new assembly shops had been built alongside the original Guy works. Hence we have the Sunbeam F4A trolleybuses supplied to Glasgow being given fleet numbers TG1-20 (trolleybus-Guy).

Guy built 315 Sunbeam trolleybuses at Fallings Park between 1953 and 1966 when the last one was built for Coimbra, Portugal. Guy had exported 10 of its prewar chassis production and 198 of the Sunbeams built at Fallings Park. So in all during 40 years a total of 811 trolleybus chassis had been built at the Guy Motors works in Fallings Park, with Wolverhampton Corporation supporting local industries by purchasing 153 of these. After Owen Silvers retired in October 1949 he became a director of the Sunbeam Trolleybus Co Ltd.

Above:
Wolverhampton starting purchasing the longer version of the Guy BTX chassis, which was suitable for a 27ft 6in-long body. No 79 was a late 1931 example. It was fitted with a Guy body which incorporated a single-step rear platform. *John Aldridge Collection*

Right:
In 1933 Guy supplied 16 of its newly-introduced two-axle BT trolleybuses to South Lancashire Transport. No 41 is caught at Atherton depot. *Metrovick/GLC*

Below:
Rotherham purchased 10 Guy BT single-deck trolleybuses in late 1933. Five were fitted with Cravens bodies and five with the only trolleybus bodies built by Roberts. No 59, one of the latter, is shown ready for dispatch from Horbury. *C. Roberts/GLC*

Right:
When Newcastle introduced trolleybuses in 1935 it acquired vehicles from three suppliers. This is one of the first 10 Guy BTX examples bought. It is seen outside the Guy works in Wolverhampton. Guy supplied 35 out of the 113 trolleybuses obtained by Newcastle prewar; only Karrier supplied more.
Guy/GLC

Below:
Also seen under Wolverhampton wires in late 1935 is Rotherham No 17. This was a Cravens-bodied 32-seat single-deck vehicle.
Guy/GLC

Right:
When Belfast chose seven manufacturers to each supply two three-axle 30ft-long trolleybuses one of the Guys was the only one to be fitted with a Park Royal body. *Dave Hurley/GLC*

Left:
After purchasing a small number of two-axle trolleybuses Wolverhampton ceased to purchase 27ft 6in-long three-axle trolleybuses in 1936 It obtained instead 26ft-long vehicles from either Guy or Sunbeam. No 263 is one of the Roe-bodied Guy BTs delivered in 1938. *Roe/GLC*

Below:
One of the Guy exhibits at the 1937 Commercial Motor Show was a BTX single-deck trolleybus fitted with a Cravens 39-seat body completed in Rotherham livery. Rotherham purchased the vehicle after the show, registering it as AET913. *Guy/GL*

Left:
Another of the Guy exhibits at the 1937 show was a two-axle BT displayed in the livery of Llanelly & District as fleet No 36. This carried a Weymann 56-seat body and was not bought by Llanelly until March 1940. In entered service in June that year registered BBX818. *John Aldridge Collection*

Right:
Guy obtained its biggest single order, for 70 chassis, from Belfast. These entered service between late 1947 and June 1949 and were numbered in the range 103 to 186. The first one completed was No 104 which is seen posing outside Stormont in October 1947. The first 26 carried the 1940 registrations originally booked for the AEC 664Ts undelivered due to the war. *Guy/GLC*

Left:
Guy's only other postwar order was for the supply of 50 8ft-wide BTs for Wolverhampton. These were fitted with Park Royal bodies. *Guy/GLC*

18 Karrier

Karrier Motors Ltd was formed in 1920 to take over the business of Clayton & Co (Huddersfield) Ltd which had in 1908 started producing 'Karrier Car' petrol-engined commercial vehicles — in Huddersfield. In 1925 the company was the first British manufacturer to build a three-axle passenger vehicle. This development was made possible by the introduction of large pneumatic tyres suitable for commercial vehicles. When Clough, Smith & Co Ltd was no longer able to purchase chassis from Straker-Squire Ltd in 1926, it turned to Karrier and entered into an agreement with them to manufacture the 'Karrier-Clough' trolley-omnibus which Clough, Smith would market.

With the drop in demand for new vehicles in the early 1930s, Tilling-Stevens Motors Ltd from Maidstone announced in July 1932 that it was taking over Karrier and moving its production to Maidstone to a new company called TS-Karrier Motors Ltd. The Karrier directors recommended the merger and the shareholders agreed. Then, in mid-September 1932, the Karrier directors withdrew from the agreement announcing 'that the firm would carry on at Huddersfield just as if the negotiations for the amalgamation had never been entered into'. The fact that Karrier was to continue in Huddersfield came as a great relief to the workforce. At the same time Huddersfield Corporation invited tenders from various manufacturers for the impending conversion of the Almondbury tram route to trolleybus operation.

In March 1933 it was announced that Clough, Smith & Co Ltd had ceased to act as sole agents for the supply of the Karrier-Clough omnibus. In future Karrier would market trolleybuses by itself. In fact the last invoice from Karrier to Clough, Smith & Co Ltd for Derby No 99, the last Karrier-Clough trolley-omnibus made, was dated October 1932.

In April 1933 Karrier received orders for three trolleybuses from Huddersfield Corporation followed by orders for Nottingham totalling 36 vehicles. This was followed by a further order for another 24 for Huddersfield. Despite this full order book the company had to appoint a receiver in June 1934. The receiver accepted the offer from Humber Ltd (part of Rootes Securities) to take over the company. By July 1935 production of the commercial vehicles had been transferred to Luton with trolleybus manufacture being moved to the Sunbeam factory in Wolverhampton, which had also been taken over by the Rootes Group in 1935. The range of Karrier trolleybuses was made here until World War 2.

Sales of Karrier trolleybuses were at this time

Below:
For Huddersfield's first trolleybus route, opened in December 1933, Karrier Motors supplied three of the six trolleybuses. No 3 was one of two Park Royal-bodied E6s. One of the pair was displayed at the 1933 Commercial Motor Show. *Karrier/GLC*

conducted from the Commer-Karrier sales offices at Biscot Road, Luton. When Huddersfield placed its order with Karrier in September 1936 for 85 trolleybus chassis it was the largest order ever placed by a municipal user with any trolleybus supplier.

The chassis numbers of the orders received at Huddersfield were in the sequence 54045-54132 for the E6 and E6A models, and 55004-55005 for the E4 model following the earlier Karrier-Clough numbers. The ones supplied via Karrier at Luton were numbered 31001-31174 for the E6 and E6A, and 30001-30052 for the E4 and E4S models. Huddersfield purchased 137 of the 262 three-axle models built. South Shields purchased 33 of the two-axle E4 model from the total of 54 built. The grand total of Karrier-designed trolleybuses was 316. The length of the bodies built on the spectacle frame E6 model was approximately 28ft 6in, with 212 being built in total. The 50 E6A models built were designed for 30ft-long bodywork and had conventional chassis frames with Kirkstall rear axles and bogie in preference to the Karrier rear axle design and spectacle frames. The E4 was designed to accept 26ft-long double-deck bodies with the two E4S being built for Darlington for 27ft 6in-long single-deck bodies. The electrical equipment for the majority of the 316 Karriers was supplied by Metropolitan-Vickers.

When the Ministry of War Transport allowed the manufacture of trolleybuses during the war, orders were placed through either Sunbeam at Wolverhampton, or with Karrier at Luton. The only model built was the W4 which was available for either single- or double-deck bodies. Of the 468 W4s built at Wolverhampton, some 199 sported Karrier badges.

After the war, orders were accepted for 34 Karrier-badged MS2s, which were on three-axle chassis, and for six Karrier-badged F4 two-axle chassis before Rootes sold the trolleybus activities to Brockhouse in 1946, with the Karrier name being retained by Rootes for use for the commercial vehicles supplied mainly to local authority users.

Left:
Doncaster, satisfied with its Karrier-Clough trolleybuses, continued to support Karrier. The chromium-plated chassis of No 32 was displayed at the 1933 Commercial Motor Show before having its Roe body fitted. *Roe/GLC*

Right:
For Huddersfield's first major tram to trolleybus conversion, the route from Waterloo to either Outlane or Lindley, Karrier supplied 24 E6s with bodies built either by Park Royal or Brush. No 16, with a Brush body, and No 21, with Park Royal, show the different interpretations of the same specification. *Karrier/GLC*

Right:
The first 30ft-long Karrier E6A trolleybuses were supplied to Newcastle in 1935. They were fitted with Metro-Cammell bodies. *Karrier/GLC*

Left:
Doncaster No 37 was a 1935 Commercial Motor Show exhibit for Karrier and was from the last batch of trolleybuses built in Huddersfield before production was moved to Wolverhampton. *Roe/GLC*

Right:
The first orders received by Rootes at Luton for Karrier trolleybuses was from South Shields, which commenced trolleybus operation in October 1936 with four E4 two-axle trolleybuses fitted with Weymann bodies. *Karrier/GLC*

HIGH VEHICLES
ALMONDBURY
TOWN CENTRE
30
Nº 115
AVH 515

Nº 116
AVH 516
HUDDERSFIELD TRANSPORT

Left:
Both the Karrier E6A test vehicles supplied to Belfast carried Harkness bodies. *Dave Hurley/GLC*

Below:
Bradford purchased from English Electric 15 Karrier E4 trolleybuses fitted with English Electric traction equipment. These were fitted with attractive 56-seat metal-framed Weymann bodies. *Dave Hurley/GLC*

Bottom:
The last genuine Karrier-designed trolleybuses were the two delivered to Darlington in August 1942. These were fitted with East Lancs 32-seat bodies. *Karrier/GLC*

Left:
The Karrier sales team at Luton continued to gain trolleybus orders from Huddersfield. In 1936 the Corporation placed orders for a total of 85 of the three-axle E6 model for completion with 28ft 4½in-long bodies. Of these, 65 were to be bodied by Park Royal and 10 each by Brush and Weymann. No 115 was numerically the last of the Brush-bodied examples. *Karrier/GLC*

Left:
The 10 Weymann-bodied examples at Huddersfield were numbered from 116, which is shown as built. Unfortunately Weymann had not realised that the position of the front axle had been moved 7in since production had left Huddersfield and, as a result, these vehicles had larger cabs than the Brush or Park Royal examples. Hence the vehicles were 29ft 2in long. The driver sat well back from the windscreen with his forward vision impaired. In an effort to correct this, new deeper windscreens had to be fitted before entering service. *Dave Hurley/GLC*

Left:
Also in 1943 South Lancs received four Karrier-badged MoWT W4 trolleybuses with Weymann 56-seat utility bodies. *Karrier/GLC*

Below left:
Huddersfield, unwilling to accept two-axle trolleybuses, had to wait until the summer of 1947 for its allocation of replacement trolleybuses for its ageing fleet. These carried basic Park Royal 70-seat bodies on Karrier-badged MS2 chassis. *Park Royal/GLC*

Below:
South Lancs had to wait until late 1948 for its six Weymann-bodied Karrier-badged MS2 chassis. No 71 (HTD868) was the last one of the six and was also numerically the last trolleybus to be purchased by South Lancs. *Metrovick/GLC*

Left:
The first Ministry of War Transport trolleybuses to be built were delivered to Darlington in early 1943. These had single-deck utility bodies built by Brush and bore Karrier builder plates. *Karrier/GLC*

Right:
Ipswich No 108 was delivered in February 1948 with wood-slatted seats in its Park Royal-built body. The chassis was a Karrier-badged MoWT W4 trolleybus. *Park Royal/GLC*

Left:
Typical of the many MoWT W4 trolleybuses fitted with Northern Coach Builders bodies, South Shields No 246 is a Karrier-badged example. *NCB/GLC*

Below:
Ipswich was the only operator to receive Karrier-badged F4 trolleybuses. This fine shot shows the final two built, Nos 113 and 114, which entered service in January 1949. These were the very last Karrier-badged trolleybuses. *Leslie Sandler*

19 Leyland

Leyland Motors Ltd established in 1907 in the Lancashire town of Leyland quickly gained a reputation for quality petrol-engined vehicles. In 1921, after the Municipal Tramways Association conference recommended the general adoption of the trolley-omnibus for tramway replacement and extensions to routes, Mr C. B. Nixon, a director of Leyland Motors Ltd, stated publicly 'that tramways should be replaced at the earliest possible moment, and as an alternative not to tinker with the trolley-omnibus but instead adopt petrol omnibuses'. Then, after an exchange of letters in the *Tramway and Railway World*, Mr Nixon concluded that 'he believed that the trackless trolley-omnibus has nearly all the disadvantages of the tram, very few of the advantages of the petrol omnibus, and that it was more expensive to install'.

Even supplying basic chassis to English Electric Ltd at nearby Preston for use in English Electric trolleybuses in the period 1926-28 did not encourage Leyland to change its opinions.

After AEC Ltd and English Electric joined forces in early 1930 to produce trolleybuses, the Birmingham-based General Electric Co Ltd, anxious to retain work for its employees and factory, persuaded Leyland to join forces with it to produce trolleybuses using Leyland chassis and GEC traction equipment.

The prototype trolleybus model TBD 1, a double-decker, was built in late 1930 and was completed in January 1931. It was basically a Leyland TD1 petrol chassis with a GEC WT25 motor of 65hp and a GEC FA3B controller fitted in place of the petrol engine. Access was gained for maintenance by removing the bonnet side. The body was built by Short Bros (Rochester and Bedford) Ltd and was of a standard Leyland lowbridge design. After initial trials on the South Lancashire system it was registered OV1175 and was tested in Birmingham for three months. After this trial period Birmingham placed an order with GEC for the supply of 11 Leyland-GEC trolleybuses. These were again type TBD1, but this time fitted with Short Bros highbridge bodies before they replaced the original 1921 Railless trolleybuses on the Nechells route in early 1932.

In May 1932 Leyland appointed Mr F. A. Garrett MIAE as manager of the newly-formed trolleybus department. Previously he had been with Ransomes, Sims & Jefferies Ltd for 10 years where he had been responsible for the development of the RSJ trolleybus.

At this point Leyland began to supply trolleybuses, with Mr Garrett responsible for a new range of

Below:
Seen in Chesterfield is the prototype Leyland-General Electric trolleybus built in 1931 which was tested extensively over the Nechells route in Birmingham, which was within two miles of the GE works at Witton where the traction equipment was made. After trials it returned to Leyland and was converted to a petrol bus, type TD1, before being sold to Jersey in February 1934. This vehicle is now preserved and has appeared on the rally scene in Halifax colours as MJX222J. It has recently been restored as Jersey J1199. *GEC/GLC*

Left:
The second prototype trolleybus built by Leyland-GEC was the TTB1, which was demonstrated in Chesterfield before going to Birmingham in March 1933 for testing on the Nechells route. It was instrumental in persuading Birmingham to purchase 50 trolley-buses with traction equipment and bodies built in the city. *John Aldridge Collection*

Right:
The third prototype trolleybus built by Leyland-GEC was a single-deck model, the TBS1. It was also fitted with a front-mounted motor. Although tested in Chesterfield, and during September 1933 at South Lancs, it does not appear to have been registered. *Leyland/GLC*

Leyland-General Electric trolleybuses with the chassis, components and the coachwork designed by Leyland Motors Ltd and the electrical equipment designed and built by the General Electric Co Ltd. The basis of these new trolleybuses was not as before a petrol bus modified to suit railless-traction work; each vehicle in the range was designed from the beginning as a trolleybus.

The range of vehicles offered included the TBS. This was a two-axle chassis which was intended primarily for a single-deck body having either central or rear entrance. However, it could still be modified, when required, for a body having a low rear platform. The TBD was a heavier two-axle chassis for double-deck bodywork and the TTB, which was a three-axle chassis suitable for double-deck bodywork for up to 66 passengers.

Leyland then built two prototype trolleybuses, one a single-deck TBS1 which was demonstrated to Chesterfield and South Lancashire Tramways, the other, a double-deck TTB1, was tested in Birmingham. The last named company, again impressed, ordered 50 of the similar TTB2 models in June 1933. This differed slightly in that the motor was mounted amidship rather than at the front as on the TTB1 and yet was still 27ft long.

The first order for the two-axle TBD2, with motor mounted amidship, was from the Llanelly & District Electrical Supply Co Ltd which ordered 14 in August 1932. Three modified TTL2 chassis, 32ft long and 8ft wide with extended chassis frames at the front were supplied to Perth, Western Australia; the first, fitted with a Leyland-built body, was tested in April 1934 over the South Lancashire Tramways system.

At the beginning of 1935, Leyland was forced to offer electrical equipment other than GEC to win orders. The first non-GEC order was for the 68 chassis produced for the London Passenger Transport Board. These received Metropolitan-Vickers equipment. During the next five years London orders had motors to either LPTB60 or LPTB70 (AMETEL) specifications. London also purchased, after demonstration, the chassisless twin steer trolleybus built in 1939.

The availability of more compact traction motors enabled Leyland to increase the wheelbase of the TTB from 16ft 6in to 18ft 7in, thereby allowing a 30ft-long body to be fitted which could carry 70 passengers and still remain within the maximum laden weights permitted.

The first of the longer examples sold was in July 1935 when the LPTB ordered 100. The first one being fitted with an all-metal body built to the requirements of the LPTB. Following this Leyland received orders for complete trolleybuses. Leyland and AEC were both favoured with large orders from London. Leyland supplied a total of 864 with 427 of them having Leyland bodies, accounting for over 50% of the 1,703 ordered by the LPTB.

When war work forced Leyland to discontinue the manufacture of passenger-carrying vehicles, Leyland had built 1,397 trolleybuses as well as supplying 17 chassis frames to English Electric. These figures make Leyland the second largest trolleybus manufacturer in the period up until 1942. This may be compared with the 1,320 chassis built by AEC in the period 1930-42 although AEC also supplied 203 sets of running units for the chassisless LPTB trolleybuses which make AEC the largest single manufacturer.

Left:
During late 1932 Leyland obtained an order from the Western Australian Government Tramways, Perth, for three TTB2 trolleybuses. These were to be 8ft wide and 32ft long with seating for 38. The first body was to be built by Leyland with the remainder being constructed in the workshops at Perth. In April 1933 the complete vehicle was tested over the South Lancs system before shipment.
Leyland/GLC

Left:
After Leyland announced that trolleybuses would be listed as standard products the first order received was in August 1932 from Balfour Beatty & Co Ltd for the supply of 14 — TBD2 — a new type of two-axle trolleybus with motor mounted centrally amidship. This time the chassis were fitted with Leyland-built bodies. *John Aldridge Collection*

Above:
In 1934 Portsmouth purchased three Leyland TBD2 trolleybuses fitted with English Electric bodies for its initial trial fleet. *EE/GLC*

Below left and below:
At the beginning of 1934 Leyland built another prototype trolleybus, model TB10. This was a revolutionary design with two traction motors, one mounted outside each chassis side frame. The chassis was completed by April 1934. After fitting with a Massey 63-seat body it was tested over the South Lancs system in February 1935. It also ran in Chesterfield later that same year. *Leyland/GLC*

Above:
In 1935 Nottingham purchased 30 Leyland TTB4 three-axle trolleybuses. These were 27ft long and were fitted with 64-seat Metro-Cammell bodies. *Ian Allan Library*

Left:
St Helens Corporation purchased a number of batches of Leyland TBD2 trolleybuses with either Brush or Massey lowbridge bodies. No 127 is a 1935 Massey-bodied example. *John Aldridge Collection*

Left:
When the London Passenger Transport Board started placing orders for trolleybuses Leyland, in March 1935, obtained the first production order for 68 of its TTB2 trolleybus chassis. Bodies were to be built by the Birmingham Railway Carriage & Wagon Co or by Brush. No 96 is one of the Brush-built examples and was photographed in February 1936. *John Aldridge Collection*

Right:
No 384, a LPTB70 model, was the first 30ft-long Leyland trolleybus supplied to the LPTB. It also carried the prototype Leyland-built all-metal body designed for 70 passengers. *John Aldridge Collection*

Left:
The South Lancashire Transport Co, after buying six TTB3s with forward-mounted motors, bought six Leyland TTB4 trolleybuses. These were 27ft long and were fitted with Roe bodies. No 54 was the first of the batch in 1938. *Roe/GLC*

Above:
Five Leyland TB3 trolleybuses were supplied to Teesside in 1936. They were fitted with Massey single-deck bodies with Edinburgh-style rear platforms. *John Aldridge Collection*

Right:
When Kingston-upon-Hull purchased its first 26 trolleybuses it chose Leyland model TB4 with Weymann 56-seat bodies. *Dave Hurley/GLC*

Left:
Manchester split its first trolleybus chassis orders between Crossley and Leyland. The latter supplied 11 30ft-long TTB6 chassis which received Manchester-built Crossley bodies on Metro-Cammell frames. In March 1938 No 1064 was 'posed' for the photographer at Higher Openshaw; hence the impossible position of the trolley booms! *Ian Allan Library*

Above:
Twelve Leyland TTB4 chassis were exported to Denmark in 1938. Five were destined for Copenhagen Tramways with the other seven for the North Zealand Tram Co (Nordsjaellands Elektricitets). The vehicles had extended chassis for the 33ft-long bodies and had the wheelbase lengthened to 18ft 7in. *John Aldridge Collection*

Right:
Leyland obtained orders from Belfast for two chassis; one was fitted with Metrovick equipment and the other GEC. When Belfast placed orders for production trolleybuses it chose GEC equipment, initially with AEC chassis and later Guy and BUT. *John Aldridge Collection*

Left:
During 1939 Leyland supplied three TB7 trolleybuses to West Hartlepool. They were fitted with Roe centre-entrance 32-seat bodies and were to become the last trolleybuses bought by the operator. *Roe/GLC*

Left:
Leyland, anxious to offer a trolleybus of chassisless construction to compete with the 175 Metro-Cammell-built examples purchased by the LPTB in late 1938, built a prototype. The Leyland approach was different to the other suppliers in that it chose a twin steering axle arrangement in an effort to avoid the severe tyre wear on the three-axle rear bogie. The LPTB purchased the demonstrator after six months' demonstration. *John Aldridge Collection*

Below:
Manchester's last Leyland trolleybus, a TB5, was No 1136. It was fitted with an English Electric-built body constructed in the West works at Preston due to the fact that the Car works (the East works) had been taken over for aircraft production for the war effort. *EE/GLC*

Above:
The last Leyland trolleybuses to enter service in London were the TTB5s diverted by the MoWT from an order due to be shipped to Durban in South Africa. A total of 25, fitted with MCW bodies, spent their lives in east London. They entered service between late 1941 and August 1942. *Ian Allan Library*

20 Railless

Railless Electric Traction Co Ltd
RET Construction Co Ltd
Railless Ltd

The Railless Electric Traction Co Ltd was registered in July 1908 to introduce the 'RET' all-British Railless Electric Traction system. It acquired the British patent rights for the Schiemann under-running trolley system which had been in use since 1901 at Bielathal in Germany. This cumbersome Railless Electric Omnibus, which looked like an old-fashioned stage coach, with large steel-tyred wheels 1.5m in diameter on the rear axle, had to be redesigned for use in Britain where rubber-tyred wheels were required. The original 20-seat design was considered by Manchester in 1908 to be too small to be commercially useful unless trailer cars were employed.

RET built an experimental car on a chassis built in London by James and Browne, it was fitted with two BTH 25hp traction motors each driving one rear wheel by chains. The body was built in Birkenhead by Milnes Voss and seated 22 inside and a further two on the rear platform. It was demonstrated at the Metropolitan Electric Tramways depot at Hendon in September 1909.

Following these trials the company vigorously promoted its system which was the only one to use overhead line equipment and trolley heads of standard tramway type. Bradford and Leeds between them purchased six trolleybuses for the first systems in this country. The chassis, built by Alldays & Onions Pneumatic Engineering Co Ltd in Birmingham, each carried two 20hp Siemens series-wound motors mounted side-by-side in the chassis frame. Again each motor drove a rear wheel by worm gearing, countershaft, sprocket and chain. The bodies were built by Hurst Nelson of Motherwell.

The various Parliamentary Bills submitted or supported by the company exhausted the company's finances and in March 1911 a new company, RET Construction Co Ltd, was formed to take over the patents, goodwill and business of the earlier company. With more financial backing it continued to promote the RET system — the Trolley Bus.

At this time Mr Edward May Munro, MIEE, MIMechE (the designer and patent holder of the trolley arms and bases used by RET), who was the Managing Director of Brecknell, Munro & Rogers Ltd of Bristol, joined the company as Chief Engineer. His assistant was Mr A. S. Crosley.

Below:
The first trolleybuses supplied by the RET Construction Co Ltd entered service in Dundee in September 1912. These had David Brown chassis frames, Siemens traction equipment and Milnes-Voss bodies. Three similar examples were supplied to Rotherham in October 1912. *GLC*

Above:
In an effort to promote trolleybuses, agencies were appointed in many overseas countries. RET formed a new company called the South American Railless Traction Co with offices in Buenos Aires and supplied it with one Milnes-Voss-bodied trolleybus in August 1913. Intended for use in Mar del Plata in the province of Buenos Aires, no evidence has been found of further vehicles being shipped there. The trolleybus is seen on test in Leeds. *GLC*

With the original Leeds and Bradford trolleybuses being over the permitted weights, the company turned to David Brown & Sons Ltd to supply lighter chassis. They continued to use Siemens traction equipment, with Milnes-Voss building the bodies. During 1912 the company acquired premises in Hunslet, Leeds, to assemble trolleybuses and carry out other work involved in the supply of complete equipment for railless electric traction. The Chief Draughtsman at the Leeds works was Charles H. Roe who, after Milnes-Voss closed its works in late 1913, designed some of the bodies using metal framing and aluminium panels which were then built next door at the premises of Lockwood & Clarkson. In October 1913 the company changed the supplier of its traction equipment to Dick, Kerr & Co Ltd of Preston and then in 1914 redesigned the transmission by fitting a new and improved chainless drive where each motor was geared to a rear wheel by one single reduction.

The company received its last three orders after World War 1 broke out. In late 1915 two more trolleybuses were delivered to Ramsbottom. Boksburg Municipality in South Africa placed a repeat order for two more in April 1915. So far, no evidence has been found to confirm whether they were delivered or not. The last order was for 10 for the North Ormesby, South Bank, Normanby & Grangetown Railless Traction Co and when in 1916 the RET Construction Co Ltd was placed in the hands of the receiver, four out of the 10 were nearly finished.

The official receiver persuaded Charles H. Roe to take over the Leeds works and set up in business as a jobbing coachbuilder. In the spring of 1918 the receiver sold the patents and goodwill of RET Construction Co Ltd to Railless Ltd, a new company owned by Short Bros (Rochester and Bedford) Ltd and manufacturing was transferred to that company's Seaplane works at Rochester, Kent. Mr E. M. Munro continued to work for the new company.

Railless Ltd completed the order for the 10 trolleybuses for North Ormesby, South Bank, Normanby & Grangetown Railless Traction Co and delivered them in August 1919. These were placed in service by the Teesside Railless Traction Board in November 1919.

The first order for the new company was received from York Corporation. Railless Ltd designed and supplied four one-man operated trolleybuses. These were only 6ft 3in wide with 24-seat bodies and entered service in December 1920. Both the Teesside and York trolleybuses have a strong resemblance to the vehicles delivered to Ramsbottom in 1915. These were fitted with C. H. Roe-designed bodies and could well have been completed by a sub-contractor for Railless.

As an aside, it should be noted that Charles H. Roe moved his bodybuilding business from Hunslet to Crossgates in 1921 having set up a limited company in May 1920. He could well have been the sub-contractor!

The next order for Railless was from Shanghai (China) for two petrol-electric trolleybus chassis, suitable for use under wires as a conventional trolleybus or for use away from the overhead using the petrol engine to drive a generator to provide electric power for the traction motor. Railless placed orders with English Electric in May 1921 for DK29B1 traction motors and DK34AS 22kW shunt wound interpole generators. The make of the petrol engine is unknown. They were fitted with electrically-operated cranes for lifting heavy weights.

About the same time Railless received orders from Bloemfontein (South Africa) for three single-deck trolleybuses and for 12 closed-top double-deck trolleybuses for Birmingham. In both cases C. H. Roe at Crossgates built the bodies. Both types were tested over the Leeds Corporation trackless routes. The first Birmingham double-decker was tried out between Guiseley and Otley on 13 July 1922. Building the Birmingham double-deckers caused severe financial problems for C. H. Roe Ltd and the company had to be refinanced as C. H. Roe (1923) Ltd. From this point Shorts built all future bodies on Railless chassis. Shorts had also been constructing all the chassis in its Rochester works since 1919.

In June 1923, Mr E. M. Munro left Railless Ltd to resume his independent consulting practice. Faced with no orders for new vehicles, Short Bros purchased

Above:
In late 1913 RET exported six trolleybuses to Boksburg to operate South Africa's first trolleybus system. These were again chain-driven from Siemens motors and were fitted with Milnes-Voss bodies. The first one is seen on test in Leeds before despatch. *GLC*

Right:
This RET open-top trolleybus was first tested in Leeds with destination blinds showing Rothwell, Wakefield, etc. This suggests that it was intended for the Morley Corporation routes that Leeds was to operate on behalf of Morley. *RET/GLC*

the balance of the share capital and reorganised the business at the end of 1923, merging the Railless sales organisation with its own to effect economics.

By July 1924 Shorts had redesigned the trolleybus for Railless Ltd who then marketed it. This completely new model had a low floor only 2ft 4in above the ground. This was achieved by fitting a special back axle with worm gearing, shaft and pinion drive to internal ring gears bolted to the brake drums. This was manufactured by Kirkstall Forge Ltd at Leeds which had supplied axles for many years to Railless. Another novel feature was brakes on all four wheels which were made from a special aluminium alloy in semi-cruciform section. The English Electric traction motors could be either single or tandem types controlled by a foot controller.

In a period of 12 months orders were received for single-deck vehicles from Ashton, Oldham, Southend and West Hartlepool, and from Nottingham, Birmingham and West Hartlepool for double-deck vehicles. The three Birmingham double-deck vehicles at 14ft 6in high were about eight inches lower than the earlier design. They were the only LF model to be fitted with hand controllers as on all other Birmingham trolleybuses at that time. All these low-floor models had an internal bodybuilder's transfer which said 'designed and built by Short Bros Rochester for Railless Ltd'.

In 1926 Short Bros decided to withdraw from building trolleybuses to concentrate on other parts of its business which were more profitable.

By then the number of known trolleybuses built were: RET Co Ltd seven; RET Construction Co Ltd 41; and Railless Ltd 67, including 28 LF models. This results in a grand total of 115.

Railless had in 1923 also granted a licence for Constructions Electriques de France at Venissieux, near Lyons, to build, for use by the Département de Gard, on a 50km route between Nîmes, Remoulins and Pont du Gard, a total of 10 tractor vehicles equipped with two motors and 35-seat bodies and also 15 single-motor goods trailers. The trolleybus train, controlled by the driver in the tractor car, had up to four trailers attached.

Below:
When RET supplied seven trolleybuses to Shanghai Electric Construction in China during 1914, they were the first to use Dick, Kerr traction equipment. They were fitted with bodies designed by the chief draughtsman, C. H. Roe, which were built by Lockwood & Clarkston in Leeds. The first examples were the last RETs to be fitted with chain drive. At least one vehicle was fitted with double basin worm driven Kirkstall axles. *RET/GLC*

Above:
When Brighton Corporation wanted to operate trolleybuses jointly with Hove, it tested the open-top double-deck RET on London Road, Brighton, in December 1913. The vehicle had been modified by moving the trolley supporting base from above the front bulkhead to above the rear bulkhead. *GLC*

Supplied by Railless Electric Traction Co

Date	Qty	Chassis	Electrical Equipment	Body builder	Customer
7/09	1	James & Browne	BTH – 2 x 25hp	Milnes Voss B24R	Hendon test vehicle
6/11	4	Allday & Onions	Siemens – 2 x 20hp	Hurst Nelson B28F	Leeds Nos 501-4
6/11	2	Alldays & Onions	Siemens – 2 x 20hp	Hurst Nelson B28R	Bradford Nos 240-1

Supplied by RET Construction Co Ltd

Date	Qty	Chassis	Electrical Equipment	Body builder	Customer
9/12	2	David Brown	Siemens – 2 x 20hp	Milnes Voss B28R	Dundee Nos 67-68
10/12	3	David Brown	Siemens – 2 x 20hp	Milnes Voss B28R	Rotherham Nos 38-40
7/13	3	David Brown	Siemens – 2 x 20hp	Milnes Voss B28R	Rotherham Nos 41-43
8/13	4	David Brown	Siemens – 2 x 20hp	Milnes Voss B28R	Ramsbottom Nos 1-4
8/13	1		Siemens – 2 x 20hp	Milnes Voss B28R	Mar del Plata, Buenos Aires
12/13	6		Siemens – 2 x 20hp	Milnes Voss B28F	Boksburg Nos 1-6
12/13	1		Siemens – 2 x 20hp	? OT40R	Brighton demonstrator No 50
6/14	6	(last chain drive)	DK26A – 2 x 20hp	Lockwood & Clarkson B28D	Shanghai
9/14	1	(first worm drive)	DK26A – 2 x 20hp	Lockwood & Clarkson B28D	Shanghai
6/15	10		DK26A – 2 x 20hp	Lockwood & Clarkson B28R	Bloemfontein Nos 1-10
6/15	5		Nil	Lockwood & Clarkson (?) (trailers)	Bloemfontein
6/15	2		DK26A – 2 x 20hp	Lockwood & Clarkson B27R	Ramsbottom Nos 5-6
/15*	10		DK26B – 2 x 20hp	Lockwood & Clarkson B28R	North Ormsby 1-10
/15**	2		DK26A – 2 x 20hp	?	Boksburg

Notes:

* This order not completed, some finished at the time the official receiver was called in when the company went into receivership in 1916. The RET works in Leeds then sold to C. H. Roe.

** This order was received in April 1915. Electrical equipment was supplied to RET but there is no evidence of the order being completed.

Supplied by Railless Ltd

Date	Qty	Chassis	Electrical Equipment	Body builder	Customer
8/19*	10		DK26B – 2 x 20hp	Railless B28R	North Ormesby Nos 1-10
12/20**	4	Model B10	DK26B – 2 x 23hp	Short B24F	York Nos 6-9
1/22	3	Model E11	DK26B – 2 x 20hp	Roe B30R	Bloemfontein Nos 16-18 (?)
7/22	1	Model H13	DK85A – 1 x 42hp	Short B?R	Ramsbottom No 7
7/22***	2	Petrol-electric trolleybus	DK29B – 1 x 60hp	Short crane lorry	Shanghai
11/22	12	Model F12	DK85A – 2 x 42hp	Roe H26/25R	Birmingham Nos 1-12
2/23	3		DK26B – 2 x 20hp	Short B30F	Ipswich Nos 1-3
12/23	4		DK85A – 1 x 42hp	Short B36F	West Hartlepool Nos 1-4

Notes:

* These had been partially built when RET Construction Co Ltd went into receivership in 1916. It is possible that the bodies were finished by Roe.

** In July 1922 Short Bros Ltd claimed the chassis and bodies were built by the company to the order of Messrs Railless Ltd.

*** These two crane lorries were fitted with petrol engines (make unknown) driving a DK34AS 22kW generator as well as 60hp DK29B traction motor.

Built under licence from Railless Ltd by Constructions Electriques de France, Venissieux, France

Date	Qty	Chassis	Electrical Equipment	Body	Customer
9/24	10	Tractor vehicle	2 x ?hp	B35F	Dept du Gard, Nîmes
9/24	15	Powered trailer	1 x ?hp	Flat platform	Dept du Gard, Nîmes

Note:
Body style similar to West Hartlepool Nos 1-4 but left-hand drive.

Supplied by Railless Ltd; Designed and Built by Short Bros All were LF model, pneumatic tyred, low-floor trolleybuses

Date	Qty	Chassis	Electrical Equipment	Body builder	Customer
7/25	8	LF30	DK99A – 2 x 35hp	Short B37C	Ashton Nos 50-57
7/25	2	LF30	DK99A – 2 x 35hp	Short B37C	Oldham Nos 1-2
10/25	2		DK85A – 1 x 42hp	Short B37C	Southend Nos 1-2
11/25*	1		DK99A – 2 x 35hp	Short H26/26ROS	1925 Commercial Motor Show exhibit
1/26	2		DK85A – 1 x 42hp	Short B36C	West Hartlepool Nos 5-6
/26**	3		DK99A – 2 x 35hp	Short H26/25ROS	Birmingham Nos 14-16
/26	1		Bull (?) – 1 x 50hp	Short OT26/22ROS	West Hartlepool No 7
/26	9		DK99A – 2 x 35hp	Short H26/26ROS	Nottingham Nos 1-9

Notes:
* Sold to Nottingham /26 as Fleet No. 10
** Only LF models to have hand operated controllers

Above:
Another export order was for the supply of 10 RET vehicles to Bloemfontein in South Africa. The order also included the supply of five trailers. *RET/GLC*

Right:
Two metal-framed trolleybuses were supplied in June 1915 to Ramsbottom Urban District Council. The bodies were again supplied by Lockwood & Clarkston. *RET/GLC*

Above:
When the RET Construction Co Ltd got into financial difficulties during World War 1, 10 trolleybuses were under construction for the North Ormesby, South Bank, Normanby & Grangetown Railless Traction Co. These were completed in 1919 by Railless Ltd for the company, which was taken over by Middlesbrough Corporation for operation by the Teesside Railless Traction Board. The TRTB was established by the corporation and by Eston UDC. *Railless/GLC*

Right:
The first new order to be obtained by Railless Ltd was for the supply of four 24-seat one-man-operated single-deck vehicles for York Corporation in 1920. The four were fitted with bodies that were only 6ft 3in wide. *Railless/GLC*

Left:
The next order was received from Bloemfontein, which took delivery of three Roe-bodied trolleybuses in 1922. *Roe/GLC*

Right:
The largest order received by Railless was from Birmingham, which took delivery in 1922 of 12 top-covered double-deck trolley-buses fitted with Roe bodywork. *Railless/GLC*

Below:
Birmingham No 11 is pictured ready for the journey from the bodybuilders using chains attached to an articulated lorry. *Roe/GLC*

Right:
Ramsbottom took delivery of a Short Bros-bodied Railless in 1922.
Railless/GLC

Above and right:
After E. M. Munro left Railless Ltd in 1923 the company was reorganised and introduced a new design of low-loading chassis. The first 10 examples went to (*Above*) Oldham (two) and (*Right*) Ashton (eight).
Railless/GLC

Above:
At the 1925 Commercial Motor Show Railless exhibited a double-deck trolleybus with a Short Bros-built open rear-staircase body intended for Birmingham Corporation, which had ordered three of the type. As a result of being fitted with a foot-operated controller it was not delivered; instead, three fitted with hand controllers were supplied. The show vehicle and nine others entered service with Nottingham. *Railless/GLC*

Below:
Also at the 1925 show was a Railless chassis which was afterwards fitted with an open-top Short Bros body. It was sold to West Hartlepool in 1926 as fleet No 7. It had a very short life, being withdrawn in 1928. *Railless/GLC*

21 Ransomes

The origin of Ransomes, Sims & Jefferies Ltd, Orwell works, Ipswich, goes back to the late 18th century when premises were acquired to carry on the business of agricultural engineers. The first involvement in passenger-carrying road vehicles was the building in 1871 of four steam coaches for the Indian Government's steam road train.

During World War 1 Ransomes started building battery-electric commercial road vehicles, marketing these as 'Orwells'. When the local council at Ipswich in September 1923 hired and placed in service three Railless trolleybuses for three months' demonstration, before applying for Parliamentary powers to convert the town's tram routes to trolleybus operation, Ransomes, and Garrett from nearby Leiston, saw a future market for trolleybuses right on the doorstep.

Ransomes designed and built an 'improved electric trolleybus', simplifying the Railless design but still using a high and straight chassis frame. They fitted a single 35hp motor driving a single worm and wheel back axle. The motor and tramway-type hand controller were built by Ransomes. The company also built the 30-seat forward-entrance body. The complete vehicle was tested and placed in service at Ipswich in 1924.

After evaluating this vehicle Ransomes designed and built a second prototype, Type C, this time eliminating the need for a three-step entrance by arranging for the floor level to be 2ft 2in above the ground. This was achieved by moving the 40hp motor to a position above the front axle. A foot-operated controller was then fitted to leave both hands of the driver free for operating the steering wheel and the emergency handbrake as well as for sounding the horn. The forward-entrance body was built by Ransomes and again it accommodated 30 passengers. In December 1925 it was loaned to Ipswich for five months until further new vehicles were available. In late 1926 it was sold to Poznan (Poland) after being fitted with pneumatic tyres and having the forward entrance repositioned on the offside.

When Ipswich placed its orders, it split them between Ransomes and Garrett, purchasing 15 Type D trolleybuses from Ransomes. Again a further design was necessary to suit Ipswich's specification of using its new trolleybuses as front entrance, one-man operated vehicles in off-peak periods and then in peak periods having the passengers use the rear entrance with a conductor collecting fares. The dual-door bodies, built by Ransomes to seat 30 passengers, had the front axle moved back. This meant that Type D had a mid-mounted motor with a higher floor level, in this case 2ft 11in.

Further variations were built to allow central-entrance bodies, different wheelbases to suit changes in length and front axle position and, as motor sizes became more compact, other variations occurred. The

Below:
Ransomes' first prototype improved trolleybus is seen on test in Ipswich during 1924 before being registered. *GLC*

first use of the D-type as a double-deck vehicle was for the two supplied to Nottingham in 1928. Also in 1928 a three-axle version, the D6-type, was introduced for both double and single-deck bodies. Again these had variable front and rear entrances to suit overseas single-deck customers.

Ransomes continued to develop and fit its own electric traction motors. The company also used its own controllers as well as fitting BTH and Allan West ones to suit clients' requirements. Gradually, however, the company withdrew from building bodies. Ransomes built up an impressive record of overseas sales, selling 305 abroad compared to only 123 home sales to 11 municipal users.

In addition, the company entered into an agreement with Stigler in Italy prior to 1935 for the latter to build, under licence in accordance with Ransomes designs, the Ransomes-Stigler six-wheel trolleybus for Milan Municipal Tramways. This was a 24-seat trolleybus which, including standees, had a capacity of 90.

The largest single order to be received by Ransomes prewar came in 1935 from Cape Town, South Africa, for 50 trolleybuses comprising 20 single- and 30 double-deck examples.

The last example sold at home was to Ipswich in 1940. This was the two-axle demonstrator, built in 1939, for a tour of South Africa which had to be cancelled due to the outbreak of World War 2.

During 1940, 14 short light type, single-deck trolleybuses were supplied to Trinidad followed, in 1941-42, by a further three diverted from Penang in Malaysia (which was then in the hands of the Japanese invaders).

After the war ended in 1945 a further 14 were built and supplied to Trinidad. These were fitted with Park Royal bodies. Then in 1946 a batch of 50 Park Royal-bodied single-deck trolleybuses were supplied to Singapore. The final six Ransomes trolleybuses were sent to Drammen (Norway) in 1948.

After this date Ransomes withdrew from trolleybus manufacture. In all, the company had built 428 and had supplied 66 out of the first 86 trolleybuses purchased by Ipswich Corporation, the operator on its own doorstep, which truly believed in supporting local industry.

Left:
The company's second prototype trolleybus, built in late 1925, was tested and used by Ipswich until the 15 production vehicles were delivered. It was then modified and sold to Poznan in Poland in 1926.
Ransomes/GLC

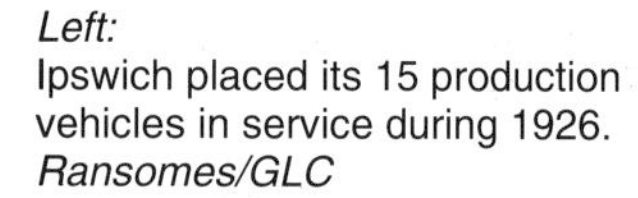

Left:
Ipswich placed its 15 production vehicles in service during 1926.
Ransomes/GLC

Right:
St Helens Corporation's first Ransomes trolleybus was delivered in July 1928.
Ransomes/GLC

Left:
In 1930, satisfied with the two 1928 Ransomes trolleybuses, Nottingham acquired six D6 three-axle trolleybuses from Ransomes. They were again fitted with Ransomes bodies. *Ransomes/GLC*

Right:
St Helens purchased five Ransomes D6 trolleybuses in 1931. They were fitted with lowbridge Ransomes bodywork. No 111 is seen on test in Ipswich. The batch was designed for use on the joint service with South Lancs.
Ransomes/GLC

Left:
Teesside RTB chose eight Ransomes for its first fleet replacements in 1932. They were fitted with rear open platform 32-seat Ransomes-built bodies. *Ransomes/GLC*

Right:
The prototype Ransomes trolleybus built in Italy under licence by Stigler was fitted with a 24-seat body. It could, however, carry 90 passengers. *Ransome/GLC*

Left:
Christchurch in New Zealand, after being supplied with a Ransomes trolleybus on free loan, purchased four Ransomes chassis. They were designed for the operator to build its own bodies before the batch entered service in 1934. *Ransomes/GLC*

Left:
Another overseas customer for Ransomes was Georgetown, Penang, which placed five orders for small light-type trolleybuses over the period from 1934 until 1941. The last order was diverted to Trinidad due to the war. *Ransomes/GLC*

Right:
The largest single order for Ransomes trolleybuses prewar was placed by Cape Town, South Africa, which received 30 double-deck and 20 single-deck trolleybuses in 1935. All were fitted with Weymann bodies. *Ransomes/GLC*

Left:
Ransomes will always be remembered for the many single-deck trolleybuses supplied to Ipswich. The last were delivered in 1930, although some still survived in service until 1954. *John Aldridge*

22 SUNBEAM

Sunbeam Motor Car Co Ltd
Sunbeam Commercial Vehicles Ltd
Sunbeam Trolleybus Co Ltd

The Sunbeam Motor Car Co Ltd, Wolverhampton, faced with falling orders for its upmarket cars, turned to making large passenger vehicles in 1929 to provide work for its factory. It introduced SMC two- and three-axle motorbuses at the 1929 Commercial Motor Show, showing its first examples of the four-wheel type SF4 'Pathan' and the six-wheel SS6 'Sikh'. Both were petrol engined. Sunbeam managed to make 15 of the SF4 and three of the SS6 model buses.

Desperate to recover its investment and seeing the success its neighbour Guy Motors was having in selling three-axle trolleybuses to Wolverhampton Corporation and other users, the company reworked one of the unsold three-axle motorbus chassis for use as a trolleybus. This was then fitted with a 70hp Metropolitan-Vickers MV110B motor, mounted centrally in the chassis, with BTH control equipment and rheostatic electric braking. All six wheels were fitted with hydraulic brakes. The double-deck body, 27ft 9½in long, was built by Weymann's Motor Bodies (1925) Ltd. It had 28 seats in the lower saloon and 33 in the upper saloon. This prototype, designated model MS1, was then placed in service at Wolverhampton for evaluation and extended trials. These trials concluded that Sunbeam had succeeded in designing a trolleybus chassis with low operating costs that would compare favourably with any other.

The Wolverhampton manager, Owen Silvers, then placed an order for three more; this time model MS2 incorporating the 70hp MV110F compound wound motor to enable regenerative braking was to be used. These vehicles, again using BTH control gear, were delivered in June 1932. After these had entered service the prototype was modified to incorporate the electrical improvements before it was purchased by Wolverhampton as an MS2.

In May 1932 Sunbeam formed a separate sales department, with Mr H. L. Brodie in charge, to market Sunbeam trolleybuses and commercial vehicles. By September 1932 Sunbeam was offering two types of four-wheel chassis — type MF1 for single-deck and type MF2 for double-deck bodies. Both were fitted with offset motors.

Meanwhile single examples of the MS2 were placed in service at Derby in October 1932, at Bournemouth in May 1933 (on 12 months' hire) and at Huddersfield in December 1933. The first large order was received from Walsall for 15 MS2 trolleybuses to be fitted with BTH201, 80hp motors.

At the 1933 Commercial Motor Show, Sunbeam showed examples of its new MS3 six-wheel chassis with offset motor and transmission to give low loading and low overall height. It also showed the new MF2A model where, by moving the motor to a position behind the front axle, a sunken gangway was possible in the lower saloon. This, combined with an offset gangway upstairs, meant that the overall height of the Park Royal body was 13ft 11in over the trolley poles at the base.

Left:
The first trolleybus produced by the Sunbeam Motor Car Co Ltd, an MS1, is pictured ready for testing in May 1931. *John Aldridge Collection*

Above right:
Sunbeam's first order was for three Type MS2 chassis with Weymann 59-seat bodies for Wolverhampton. *Dave Hurley/GLC*

Right:
When Bournemouth's experimental route opened in May 1933 this Sunbeam MS2, registered LJ7701, was one of the four vehicles hired. *Ian Allan Library*

In January 1934 after eight months' trial of varying types, Sunbeam was chosen by Bournemouth to supply its first fleet of 12 vehicles. This was followed in early 1934 by the receipt of the company's first export order — from South Africa — where Durban ordered 11 MF2 models.

From mid-1933 Sunbeam had advertised that all its trolleybuses had electrical traction equipment manufactured by the British Thomson-Houston Co Ltd (BTH). Following this date all Sunbeam trolleybuses were advertised as Sunbeam-BTH models.

During 1934 Sunbeam had invested £3.5 million on a new motorcar model, which was intended to be a money-maker. Unfortunately sales did not justify the investment and it practically bankrupted the company. In an effort to separate the trolleybus activities from the car side, on 17 November 1934 a new company, Sunbeam Commercial Vehicles Ltd, was formed. By then Sunbeam had built or had on order 136 six-wheel and 18 four-wheel trolleybuses, including at least 84 still to be delivered to Bournemouth. Total orders from this south coast operator reached 103 of the MS2 model, making it the largest user of Sunbeam trolleybuses before World War 2.

Even with this full order book for trolleybuses the losses in the car business put the company in the red and in July 1935 the business and assets were sold to Rootes Securities. The new owner stopped car production at Wolverhampton, whilst at the same time transferring the trolleybus manufacture of the recently-acquired Karrier Motors Ltd business to Wolverhampton. This concentrated the manufacture on one site of two manufacturers' products, although these continued to be marketed separately.

In December 1935 AEC gained a financial interest in the company with both J. T. C. Moore-Brabazon and C. W. Reeve (AEC's chairman and managing director respectively) joining the Board. Sunbeam Commercial Vehicles still continued to offer MF1, MF2, MF2A, MS2 models and introduced the MF3. This was a lightweight trolleybus for overseas use intended for 24-seat lightweight bodies with a 35hp motor. Also introduced was the MF3A with the front axle set back to allow a front entrance. The MF3 and MF3A were intended for the former customers of the AEC 603 model. At the same time a Karrier version

Left:
Sunbeam's first two-axle trolleybus, a MF2A, was fitted with a Park Royal lowbridge body that was only 13ft 11in high over the trolley poles at the base. It was displayed at the 1933 Commercial Motor Show.
Dave Hurley/GLC

Left:
The company's second two-axle trolleybus was an MF1, which was sold to Wolverhampton with a 34-seat Park Royal body in 1934.
Dave Hurley/GLC

was offered as the E4L. To compete with other manufacturers SCV introduced the 18ft 6in-long wheelbase version of the MS2 for 30ft-long, 70-seat bodies.

In 1937 a range of battery-electric vehicles was introduced which included the MB for up to 15 seats and the MB1 for 22 seats. Again BTH motors and control gear were fitted. At least one 13-seat passenger-carrying example was built for use on the pier at Weston-super-Mare, where it had advantages over most other types of passenger vehicles. On the pier it did not have to be licensed!

In 1939 the MS2C was introduced and Rotherham purchased a total of 15. This was the first SCV model to be fitted with a GEC type WT268E, 107hp traction motor. Rotherham, at that time, operated the fastest scheduled trolleybus services in Britain.

In October 1939 SCV announced the receipt of an order for 25 8ft-wide MF2 models for shipment to Johannesburg. Unfortunately, due to the war and lack of shipping facilities, these were never dispatched. In 1942 the Ministry of War Transport arranged for these to be allocated to the municipalities of Bradford, Nottingham and St Helens.

At this point SMC and SCV had built a total of 368 trolleybuses comprising 248 three-axle and 120 two-axle vehicles. Of these 128 were exported with 85 of the 240 UK examples serving the citizens of Wolverhampton, even if some of this total ran in from Walsall on a joint route.

When the Ministry of War Transport allowed Sunbeam and Karrier to build the W4 model (wartime, four-wheels) for the trolleybus needs of wartime Britain, one basic product was produced incorporating the salient features of the Karrier E4 and the Sunbeam MF2 two-axle types. The 26ft-long double-deckers were built on chassis with a wheelbase of 16ft 3in. This was extended for the single-deck version. Various makes of traction equipment were used. After AEC withdrew its interest, Rootes sold the company in July 1946 to Brockhouse & Co Ltd. In June 1948 the company was renamed the Sunbeam Trolleybus Co Ltd which was then sold to Guy Motors Ltd in October 1948. Guy Motors then ceased to market its own range of trolleybuses; instead it concentrated on promoting the Sunbeam range which included: the F4 and F4A, (two-axle 26ft, 27ft and 30ft-long double-deck); the S7 and S7A (three-axle 30ft and 33ft 6in-long double-deck); and the MF2B (available in various lengths up to 36ft long, intended as an overseas transit chassis but used in the UK for double-deck applications at Hull and Bournemouth).

Right:
At the 1933 Commercial Motor Show one of the five Weymann-bodied Sunbeam MS2 trolleybuses ordered by Walsall was displayed. Unlike the Birmingham exhibit, which had a single-step platform, Walsall chose a two-step arrangement. *Dave Hurley/GLC*

Above:
Wolverhampton bought all but two of the Sunbeam MS3 double-deck trolleybuses built. No 98 is one of the five purchased in early 1934. One of the batch appeared at the 1933 Commercial Motor Show. They were fitted with Metro-Cammell bodies. *BTH/GLC*

Right:
Bournemouth No 72, the first of 12 Sunbeam MS2 trolleybuses, was one of six fitted with Park Royal dual entrance/exit bodywork. It was supplied in 1934. *BTH/GLC*

The postwar trolleybuses could be fitted with a choice of electrical equipment from British Thomson-Houston Co Ltd, Crompton-Parkinson Ltd, General Electric Co Ltd or Metropolitan-Vickers Electrical Co Ltd.

Production was moved to the Guy works at Fallings Park in 1953 after suitable accommodation had been built. The works at Moorfields was then sold. Some 1,541 trolleybuses had been built there including 465 Karriers. Fallings Park continued to build trolleybuses until 1966 when the last one was built for Coimbra, Portugal. By this time 315 Sunbeams had been built there comprising 65 F4A, 40 S7 and S7A models and 210 MF2Bs. By then, 1,391 Sunbeam-badged trolleybuses had been made and, if one adds the Karrier production, the total is 1,856.

Left:
Sunbeam supplied two MS2 trolleybuses to Belfast in 1938. These were fitted with all-metal Cowieson bodies. *Sunbeam/GLC*

Left:
Wolverhampton No 242 was a 1936 Sunbeam MF2 fitted with a Park Royal body. *Dave Hurley/GLC*

Below left:
Walsall No 178, a 1938 Sunbeam MS2, is shown ready for towing from the bodybuilder — Park Royal — with the half shafts removed. *Dave Hurley/GLC*

Right:
Rotherham No 70 was the prototype Sunbeam MS2C chassis and was fitted with a 107hp GEC motor. In entered service in October 1940 fitted with an East Lancs body. *BTH/GLC*

Below right:
Teesside No 14 was the only Sunbeam MF2A chassis fitted with a single-deck body. It was new in 1942 and the body was supplied by East Lancs. *BTH/GLC*

Left:
World War 2 caused 26 Sunbeam MF2 chassis intended for Johannesburg to be reallocated by the Ministry of War Transport. Ten of them, fitted with 8ft-wide lowbridge bodies by Massey, went to St Helens. *Sunbeam/GLC*

Below:
Ashton No 66 was a Sunbeam W4 trolleybus that was delivered in early 1946. It was fitted with a Roe utility body. *Metrovick/GLC*

Right:
Newcastle's first two-axle Sunbeam trolleybuses were 35 F4s delivered in 1949. They carried attractive Metro-Cammell bodies and had the distinction of being ordered from Rootes in May 1946 as Karrier F4s. No 468 was shown at the 1948 Commercial Motor Show. *Metrovick/GLC*

Below:
The only Sunbeam-badged MS2 trolleybuses to be supplied postwar to a British operator were those sold to Huddersfield between 1949 and 1951. The last 14 carried Roe 70-seat bodies. No 593 was an exhibit at the 1950 Commercial Motor Show. *Roe/GLC*

Right:
Sunbeam's postwar three-axle design was the S7. The type first appeared at Newcastle in 1948. The corporation placed 30 in service with 70-seat Northern Coach Builders bodywork. Similar vehicle No 512 was displayed at the 1948 Commercial Motor Show. *Sunbeam/GLC*

Above:
In 1950 Reading placed 12 Sunbeam S7 trolleybuses in service. They were fitted with 8ft-wide 68-seat Park Royal bodies complete with platform doors.
Ian Allan Library

Left:
The last F4 Sunbeam trolleybuses built were the 20 supplied to Derby in late 1952/early 1953. These were fitted with Willowbrook 60-seat bodywork. Originally these had been ordered with Brush bodywork, but due to a change of policy at Brush coachwork orders were transferred to Willowbrook. Willowbrook had previously built, in 1937 on the Daimler prototype, only a single trolleybus body. *BTH/GLC*

Right:
Glasgow selected the Sunbeam F4A for its first 20 two-axle double-deck trolleybuses. No TG1 (Trolleybus Guy 1) entered service in 1953; it was the first of only five trolleybuses to carry Alexander bodywork. The seating capacity was 62. *GLC*

Above:
Glasgow's other 15 F4As carried 62-seat Weymann bodies. *EE/GLC*

Above:
At the 1952 Commercial Motor Show G. H. Pulfrey, the enterprising General Manager at Hull, displayed a revolutionary trolleybus for Britain. This was a Sunbeam MF2B chassis fitted with a forward-entrance/centre-exit 54-seat Roe body. This 1953 view shows No 101 being tested by Metrovick engineers. A further 15 of the type, known as the 'Coronation' type, were delivered in 1954-55. It had been Pulfrey's intention to use them for one-man operation and, as a result, all were fitted with trolley retrievers. This made them the most advanced trolleybuses to be used in Britain. *Metrovick/GLC*

Below:
In 1954 the equally enterprising General Manager of Walsall, R. Edgley Cox, obtained dispensation from the Ministry of Transport to operate 30ft-long two-axle trolleybuses using extended Sunbeam F4A chassis with 70-seat Willowbrook bodies. The first one, No 851, was shown at the 1954 Commercial Motor Show. Eventually a total of 22 were purchased. *BTH/GLC*

Below:
Bournemouth purchased 40 Sunbeam MF2B chassis in the period from 1958 until 1962. Unfortunately one was destroyed at the Weymann factory whilst under construction. These vehicles still retained rear-entrance open platforms with front exit. When, in October 1962, Bournemouth received No 301 it was to be the last trolleybus to be delivered to a British user. *C. Carter*

Above:
In 1958 Belfast, considering the replacement of its fleet with new vehicles, bought its one and only 30ft-long two-axle trolleybus. The Sunbeam F4A was fitted with a 68-seat Harkness body. *Author*

Below:
In 1961 Reading Corporation purchased 12 Sunbeam F4A 30ft-long trolleybuses fitted with Burlingham forward-entrance bodies and platform doors. Six of the batch were supplied with refurbished motors and electrical equipment from withdrawn Reading trolleybuses.This was one of five sold to Teesside in 1969. *Ian Allan Library*

23 Thornycroft

John I. Thornycroft & Co Ltd of Basingstoke, a well-known supplier of petrol-engined chassis for road use, was one of the country's more unusual trolleybus manufacturers.

An advertisement in 1923 for the company's products included a photograph of a Type J trolley-omnibus supplied to Shanghai. There is no reference to this in the company records but examination of the English Electric Co Ltd records show that in October 1921 Matheson & Co Ltd placed an order for 14 sets of traction equipment comprising DK85A 40hp motors and SE1 type controllers. They were to be shipped to Shanghai before the end of 1921. By April 1922 an article in *Tramway and Railway World* described the latest railless trolley cars built by Shanghai Electric Construction Co Ltd for itself to the instructions of its engineer Mr Donald McColl. One of the illustrations in the article was used in the 1923 advertisement.

In 1924 the technical press, reviewing progress made by Thornycroft and its involvement in the Far Eastern market, gave details of a new development for the company. It had supplied a railless trolley car for service at Georgetown in the Malay Peninsula. The body built by Strachan & Brown seated 28. It was fitted with a BTH motor and equipment and was claimed to be the first trolleybus to be fitted with pneumatic tyres. Records show this to be chassis No 9839X, built in May 1924. This was followed in December 1924 by the building of two BT model trolleybuses, chassis Nos 11434 and 11435. These were supplied with trailers and were described as 'Shanghai type railless engines'.

Another puzzle exists with English Electric records showing one set of traction equipment being delivered in June 1922 to Thornycroft works on behalf of Shanghai Tramways, on a sale or return basis. This comprised one DK85A motor and a foot-operated controller type EMB RT1, these parts being returned to Preston with the comment 'No Sale'.

These are the only definite references to Thornycroft-supplied trolleybuses. However, in 1930 the company started to supply chassis assemblies to Brush Electrical Engineering Co Ltd for use in the Brush-Thornycroft trolley-omnibuses marketed by Brush. This venture did not flourish and, after three had been built, it died.

Thornycroft had difficulties in the 1930s getting orders and failed to make much progress with its passenger range of vehicles although it was offering 40 different civilian goods models in 1932.

Above:
The first complete Thornycroft trolleybus was supplied in 1924. It was fitted with a Strachan & Brown body and became Georgetown's second trolleybus. *Thornycroft/GLC*

Left:
Thornycroft was advertising in 1923 that this Thornycroft J trolleybus was operating in Shanghai, China. What the company did not admit was that it had been built by the user on a J type chassis with the traction equipment being purchased from English Electric by a company in Shanghai. *Thornycroft/GLC*

24 Tilling-Stevens

Tilling-Stevens Motors Ltd of Maidstone was formed in 1912 when Thomas Tilling joined forces with the Maidstone company of W. A. Stevens Ltd to manufacture petrol-electric motorbuses which were simple to drive. As the vehicle had no clutch or gearbox it was easy to train former horsebus drivers to drive motorbuses. Many hundreds of vehicles were built and supplied to loyal users. One of these customers, Wolverhampton Corporation, first operated the type in 1917 and when in 1923 the general manager, Owen Silvers, recommended replacing trams on the Wednesfield route with trolley vehicles he chose, after careful consideration of available vehicles, Tilling-Stevens as the supplier. The model chosen was a trolleybus version of the Tilling-Stevens TS6 petrol-electric motorbus. It was fitted with a tandem motor comprising two armatures each rated at 25hp, mounted on the same shaft and controlled by a BTH foot-operated controller. The first six were placed in service in late 1923.

In 1924 Halifax Corporation Tramways purchased a 2 to $2^1/2$-ton chassis from Tilling-Stevens fitted with two 25hp motors for use on their one trolleybus route.

This was followed in July 1924, when the Teesside Railless Traction Board placed in service a vehicle unique to Britain: its designation was Petrol Electric Railless Chassis 1 (PERC 1). It was built by Tilling-Stevens to instructions from Mr J. B. Parker, the TRTB General Manager, who had designed and patented it. Basically it was a standard TS3A petrol-electric chassis which could operate from the overhead wires or be driven independently by the petrol engine driving the dynamo to provide current for the traction motor.

In 1925 a TS6 trolleybus was placed in service at Ipswich for evaluation against other makes.

During late 1926 W. A. Stevens advised Owen Silvers, the Wolverhampton Manager, on adapting Guy three-axle motorbus chassis into trolleybuses using traction motors incorporating Rees-Stevens patents.

Above:
Wolverhampton's first trolleybus in 1923 was supplied by Tilling-Stevens and was fitted with a Dodson body. *BTH/GLC*

In the period from 1927 to 1929 Tilling-Stevens continued to offer two-axle trolleybus chassis fitted with either tandem or single motors suitable for 56-seat double-deck bodies but was unable to sell any. By this date Tilling-Stevens had built 35 single-deck trolleybuses including the PERC 1; 32 were supplied to Wolverhampton, with the last one being supplied with a drop frame for a lower saloon floor.

Although the manufacture of petrol-electric chassis had practically ceased by 1927 with the company producing a range of conventional petrol-engined chassis, Tilling-Stevens purchased the patent rights

from Mr J. B. Parker after receiving enquiries from abroad for petrol-electric trolleybuses.

The Tilling empire embraced many motorbus operating companies who were finding that Tilling-Stevens vehicles were underpowered compared with those of other manufacturers, Thomas Tilling in July 1930 withdrew from the partnership and started buying most of its vehicles from other manufacturers.

A new company T. S. Motors was formed to carry on the business at Maidstone. Faced with a falling order book the company looked elsewhere for new customers. With the Royal Commission on Transport predicting that municipal undertakings would be turning to the trolleybus as a replacement for the tram, TSM Ltd built and exhibited at the 1930 Scottish Motor Show a combined petrol-electric and trolleybus chassis, which, due to its weight, was suitable only for single-deck bodywork. The chassis was tested on the Maidstone trolleybus routes.

The only sale made was to Turin, Italy, in late 1931, for experimental use. It was fitted with a Short Bros (Rochester and Bedford) body with 23 seats and provision for 25 standees. This was the only left-hand drive example built, being converted from the exhibition chassis.

In July 1932 in an effort to find work for its Maidstone factory, T. S. Motors entered into an agreement to acquire Karrier Motors Ltd and move its production to Maidstone. However, in September 1932 the Karrier directors withdrew from the agreement in order to keep production in Huddersfield. In 1938 the company was successful in acquiring the Vulcan Motors & Engineering Co Ltd from Southport and moved production to Maidstone. In 1949 T. S. Motors Ltd was finally taken over by Rootes Securities.

Above:
The Teesside Tilling-Stevens petrol-electric trolleybus was fitted with a Roe body and was built in 1924. *Ian Allan Library*

Left:
The last Tilling-Stevens trolleybus supplied in 1925 to Wolverhampton had similar Dodson bodywork, but the chassis frame was lowered to give a two-step entrance. *John Aldridge Collection*

Above:
The 1930 Scottish Motor Show exhibit for T. S. Motors was this petrol-electric trolleybus chassis. *John Aldridge Collection*

Right:
After the show the chassis was converted to normal control and fitted with a Short Bros body for export to Turin in Italy. *John Aldridge Collection*

25 Trackless Cars

(Known earlier as the Electric Traction Co)

Trackless Cars Ltd, whose registered office was at Hepworth Chambers, Briggate, Leeds, was responsible for selling railless trolley tractors built to the Bishop and Chadwick patents in the early 1920s. These patents revolved around a front-wheel drive system, in which the fore-carriage contained two motors, one in front of the axle and one behind. Each motor drove one of the front road wheels by a pinion on the motor shaft and an internal ring gear fixed in the wheels. The steering wheel rotated the whole fore-carriage with the disadvantage that some 36 revolutions of the steering wheel were necessary to effect a U-turn at the terminus.

The first railless vehicle using this system was placed in service in Leeds in January 1920 and proved to be satisfactory. Leeds was impressed and signed an agreement in June 1920 for up to 30 cars to be rebuilt in this manner using Mr G. A. Bishop's patent.

In January 1921 the Keighley manager asked for that operator's trackless No 58 to be rebuilt to front-wheel drive, retaining the Cedes motors. Expensive jigs and patterns had to be made and the original estimate of £700 was soon exceeded and the conversion eventually cost £2,184. The work was competed in August 1921.

Meanwhile in October 1921 Leeds introduced the first of three low-height double-deck Railless Trolley Tractors. Through the use of a drop frame behind the fore-carriage, the height to the top of the canopy was only 13ft 10in. This allowed the vehicles to pass under a 14ft 6in railway bridge. The saloon floor of the railless was only 1ft 8in above the road surface. Leeds built the bodies in tramway style, at its Kirkstall Road works, to carry 59 passengers and also assembled the three chassis which were designed under the watchful eye of the Electric Traction Co's engineer Mr J. Wright. Inspired by the success so far, Trackless Cars built its next vehicle, a 64-seat, double-deck car, with a 15ft 0in wheelbase. This was of revolutionary design, incorporating a central entrance with platform doors, a central staircase and again was the same overall height of 13ft 10in. The body was built in Leeds by the Blackburn Aeroplane & Motor Co Ltd at its Olympia works in Roundhay and was 24ft 11in long. The electrical equipment was ordered through Tramway Supplies Co Ltd, Leeds, and comprised two DK26B 20hp motors, a Type D controller and Maley resistance.

It was demonstrated to the Tramway Congress at

Above:
Keighley asked Trackless Cars to rebuild its Cedes-Stoll No 58 to front-wheel drive incorporating the original Cedes Hub motors. It finally re-entered service in August 1921. *Keighley News/GLC*

Left:
Leeds No 510, the first of the three Trackless Cars trolley tractors fitted with bodies built by Leeds Corporation at its Kirkstall Road Works, was built in 1921 and, after initial testing on the Farnley route, was transferred in early 1922 to the Guiseley-Otley route where it gave good service. *GLC*

Left:
Leeds Railless No 503 (U8405), a trolleybus dating originally from 1911, was reconstructed with a new Leeds-built body powered by the prototype front-wheel drive Trackless trolley tractor. It re-entered service in January 1920. *GLC*

Right:
Leeds No 513, the third Trackless Cars low-height double-deck trolley tractor, entered service in January 1923. *GLC*

Bournemouth in June 1922 and then in July 1922 to the London Underground Group at Twickenham. It was finally purchased by Leeds in January 1924.

Whilst the design had many advantages — low height, ease of access, readily replaceable fore-carriage which could be completely replaced in two hours so avoiding lengthy absence from service — the obvious disadvantage was the number of turns necessary on the steering wheel to avoid other vehicles. The driver must have been exhausted by the end of each shift.

No more Railless Trolley Tractors were built and by February 1926 the last survivor was withdrawn from service.

Above:
Trackless Cars built a demonstration double-deck vehicle with a centre door and staircase body built by the Blackburn Aeroplane & Motor Co at the latter's Olympia works in Roundhay, Leeds. It is shown being prepared to be towed to Bournemouth in June 1922. *Blackburn Aeroplane & Motor Co/GLC*

Left:
In January 1924 Leeds purchased the Trackless Cars demonstrator and placed it in service as fleet No 513 after fitting front windows to the upper deck. *GLC*